"I am so delighted by this book! While a lot of resources can help you create a pretty and stylish home, Courtney will help you create a meaningful and memorable home, one that honors the people and stories it holds while creating space for connection and new experiences. Also, she's really funny and her book is so enjoyable to read. You'll want to start a project the moment you put it down!"

Lindsay Sherbondy, owner and artist at Lindsay Letters Co.

"Courtney Warren makes the challenge of weaving style and personality into your home fun, budget-friendly, and easy to achieve. This book holds all her tips for creating a lifestyle that looks as beautiful as if feels and encourages personal touches that make every room truly custom. As someone who has worked firsthand with Courtney, I can tell you that the tips in this book are exactly what she used to create a space we are in love with."

Hilary Kennedy, TV host and influencer

"Courtney Warren is the decorating girlfriend we all need—honest, quirky, and full of surprising and out-of-the-box ideas. *The Story of Your Home* will help you find your unique style, add your own personal touches to the rooms you love, and find joy in the midst of an imperfect but perfect-for-you home. Whether you're decorating a rental or your forever home, you'll find visual inspiration, surprising ideas, and empathetic coaching within its pages."

Mary DeMuth, author of 46 books,
including *The Wall Around Your Heart*

"Courtney Warren is truly the most inspiring designer who freely shares her expertise with all of us. Her new book, *The Story of Your Home*, is fueled with a passion for design and includes action steps to help anyone get started. You can find plenty of books that will tell you how to design something, but rarely does an author take the time to add such detailed quizzes, questionnaires, and starting points as Courtney. This book is an absolute MUST-HAVE for anyone with a desire to turn their house into a home. I cannot wait to apply the things I have learned from Courtney!"

Kelly Ballard, entrepreneur and DIY decorating blogger at *City Girl Meets Farm Boy*

"Keep your highlighter in arm's reach because this gem is chock-full of practical steps to solve the trickiest decor problems. Courtney's voice is relatable, fun, and authentic. By the end of the book, I felt both equipped to tackle my decor issues and refreshed by Courtney's encouragement and humor."

Wendy Zock, DIY and design blogger at *The Curated Farmhouse*

THE STORY OF YOUR HOME

THE STORY OF YOUR HOME

A Room-by-Room Guide to Designing
with Purpose and Personality

Courtney Warren

Revell
a division of Baker Publishing Group
Grand Rapids, Michigan

© 2023 by Courtney Warren

Published by Revell
a division of Baker Publishing Group
Grand Rapids, Michigan
www.revellbooks.com

Printed in China

Library of Congress Cataloging-in-Publication Data
Names: Warren, Courtney, author.
Title: The story of your home : a room-by-room guide to designing with purpose and personality / Courtney Warren.
Description: Grand Rapids, MI : Revell, a division of Baker Publishing Group, [2023] | Includes bibliographical references.
Identifiers: LCCN 2022032660 | ISBN 9780800742102 (cloth) | ISBN 9781493441440 (ebook)
Subjects: LCSH: Interior decoration—Psychological aspects.
Classification: LCC NK2113 .W37 2023 | DDC 747—dc23/eng/20220719
LC record available at https://lccn.loc.gov/2022032660

Some names and details have been changed to protect the privacy of the individuals involved.

Principal photography by Jarred Estes

Photography by Mandy Mann on page 13; Shannon Williams at Overflow Creative Studio on pages 77, 134, and 175; Paula Waters on page 110; Chris Tucker on pages 129, 141, 145, and 148; and Mike Davello on page 193 (left)

Published in association with Books & Such Literary Management, www.books andsuch.com.

Interior design by Jane Klein

Baker Publishing Group publications use paper produced from sustainable forestry practices and post-consumer waste whenever possible.

23   24   25   26   27   28   29   7   6   5   4   3   2   1

Dedicated

to my boys, Judah and Abe.
You are my favorite story.

In memory of

my grandmother Helen,
who used her natural talents
to create the loveliest home
in the neighborhood, filled
with warmth and love—
all with an eighth grade
education and no interior
design training.

Contents

Introduction

What Informs Your Current Story

HELLO FRIEND, walk with me. I'm thrilled you made it—you're right on time. As an interior designer, I am frequently asked hot-button questions, so today I am speaking on a panel to answer them, and I would like you to be my honored guest. Snacks are to the right and the espresso machine is in the Green Room. Please hang out here. I'm being called to the panel, but I'll be right back to show you around.

(Cue the sounds of a packed room, flashing cameras, background murmurs, and crowds clamoring to get their burning questions answered.)

Q: Courtney, Courtney, over here! Where do I stop painting when I have an open floor plan?

A: Hi there, you with the nice green eyes. Find a natural stopping place. For instance, where walls meet each other. If that spot is hard to find, you may have to paint the entire space until you come across a natural ending point. Sometimes this means painting the tall ceilings of a foyer or wall upstairs in an open entry.

Q: Courtney! Over here! Can I mix metals and wood finishes?

A: Hello, you in the clown suit. Yes, it's actually ideal. If everything matches too much, the room might give off a "showroom of a big box store" kind of vibe. Combining a few contrasting finishes will actually complement each other and also provide variation.

Q: Courtney, Courtney, help save my marriage! How do we achieve peace when my spouse and I have drastically different design tastes?

A: Let's go to the lovely lady in the corner who "put a ring on it." When your spouse is more passionate than you about the subject, you've found a natural place where you can easily give in. When you're both equally invested in the matter, try to find an area to meet in the middle. Past that, seeking an impartial third opinion is immeasurably helpful. This needs to be a neutral party—not a friend or it's hardly impartial. Above all, remember that people are more important than things. If this decision causes any sort of rift in your relationship, I suggest you honor the person over the design.

Q: My turn! Do any of your other clients want to buy this piece of furniture that I am discarding?

Someone pipes up in the back: "Yeah. I paid a lot for a piece I don't need anymore, and I want to make my money back."

A: Okay, the last question goes to the man in the round glasses who is awkwardly cradling an oversized adding machine like a baby. Let me answer your question with a question. Sir, did you use the item? Did it serve you well? Furniture is not usually an investment outside of comfort and beauty. Rarely will someone recoup the initial cost for the item. Which is logical, since the items you are done with are outdated, so you might guess that other people desire a similar upgrade. I see the phases very clearly when I visit clients. Everyone is attempting to part with the same style that was popular ten years ago. There is not a big market for outdated furniture, no matter the origin or the original price. If a piece served you well, rest assured that you got your money's worth, and it is acceptable to let it go guilt-free. If you really want to bless someone, pay it forward to a young couple starting their journey or a single parent struggling to make ends meet.

(End scene.)

While that scenario was born of my imagination, these are the most frequently asked questions I hear, along with others I answer throughout this book. Yet there is one topic that is broached repeatedly, and it happens to be quite controversial for some designers. In fact, if you even *attempt* to mention this in a room of design professionals, you'll probably see every head swivel in your direction and give you the stink eye. Suddenly the dangerous biker gang from *Peewee's Big Adventure* will surround you, scowling and pounding their clenched fists into the open palms of the opposite hand—a gesture oddly used only in movies.

What topic could invite such scorn? What issue could possibly stir such controversy? TV size? Throw pillow positioning? Thermostat settings!?!

Folks, it is reality TV.

THINGS ON TV ARE NOT HOW THEY APPEAR

If you desire to start a real minor controversy, confide in a designer that you want to achieve decor perfection with the same tight timeline and minuscule budget you saw on TV. Then bring some popcorn, prop your feet up, and get ready to hear most designers deliver a sermon that will deserve your Sunday best.

The honest truth is that what we observe on TV is not exactly how things work. I realize it is *called* reality TV, but that is as accurate as informing your kids that you are having a "discussion" with your spouse when everyone knows it's a fight. "True adjacent" at best might be more apt a description.

I am not trying to insinuate that designers are opposed to home shows. I personally would love to host my own show one day. Perhaps one called *Reveal* where we showcase only before and afters, because that is what we're really watching to see. However, some design professionals would contend that the renovation process on design series is accelerated, inaccurate, and simplified to fit the network's needs. Since many folks tend to believe what they see on TV, who gets to break the bad news that the update will cost more time and money in the real world? You got it!

The designer. Hooray! The project hasn't even started and we are already disappointing our clients. Just as in real life, six-packed bachelors do not loiter in the tropics until the subsequent make-out session with the next marriage-ready bikini model, and most renovations do not follow the same exact formula demonstrated on-screen.

When I was cast for an episode of a design-themed TV show, I was quickly educated on how much "reality" actually comprises reality TV. For instance, some reality shows follow participants "shopping" for houses, but a peek behind the curtain reveals that buyers usually have already located and purchased their property. The network simply stages the search to set up the story for the viewers' entertainment and for the foundation of the episode. Translated, normal people re-create or reimagine a situation to entertain us. Another word for that is *acting*. Now, I realize the suggestion that our beloved makeover shows are not 100 percent truth might feel like I informed you Santa did not make all your toys, but before we label a show as "fake" too quickly, let's consider what it would look like if renovations were based on reality. We would likely flip the channel. We would literally be watching paint dry. Do we really want to see real time delays, returns, and mistakes? These shows do not exist to educate us on how the design industry works any more than *The Bachelor* explains how dating works.

So, the next time you try to apply your real-life rules to what you see on the screen, please remember that objects on TV are not always as they appear.

Occasionally, after I share home photos on my Instagram feed (@CourtneyWarren), my online community confesses that they cannot keep their house as tidy as I do every day. Then I divulge the truth—I can't either. My real house is not as clean as my "online house."

Do you believe what you see on social media is how people really live? You might jump to say, "No, of course not!" but if you were splayed out on the social media X-ray table and searched with a wand that looked for comparison envy, would it beep?

I have never cleaned as much as the days *Better Homes & Gardens* and TLC came to film my house. I scoured every inch of every surface—even those that would never possibly be discovered. I could have started a basketball team with the dust bunnies I found under my bed. Why did I clean under my bed? I have no idea, because no one came even close to that dark abyss where things go to die. But just in case they wanted to feature a sidebar about what I store beneath my bed, I stood ready.

(Interestingly enough, readers, you will never guess what Courtney Warren, the Texas Interior Designer, keeps under her bed. All her lost hairbands. Upon further review, she also has eye drops, pens, a dog-eared copy of *Boundaries* by Henry Cloud, and a left flip-flop that's been missing since last summer. You heard it here first!)

My home has never been as spotless as the days the cameras popped in, and it will likely never be that neat again. Right now, I am pretty sure a mushroom is attempting to take possession of my kid's closet and become his leader. Am I going to post that mess online? Heck no. Would you?

Which brings us to another behind-the-scenes fact: most online influencers clean their house, take a slew of photos, and then use them to make different posts throughout the month. This exercise is so common it even has a name—*batching*. Batching is a social media planning practice that saves people the effort of planning content for many posts at the same time. The photos you see might have been taken last month, last quarter, or even last year. Because influencers also live in their homes. They have evidence of muddy footprints and dog vomit, and they probably occasionally eat pizza on paper towels instead of a real plate.

What you see on TV, in magazines, and on social media is a snapshot, only curated for entertainment. I have heard this concept extolled so frequently it might seem rote, but sometimes that repetition may never reach our hearts. It's a universal struggle that I have to remind myself of and want to encourage you with—please do not allow the online examples of perfection to make you feel unsatisfied in your home.

Social media and TV paint a picture for entertainment purposes, and the picture is not reality. Let this be your line in the sand, or perhaps, more realistically, if you're like me, a line through the dust bunnies under the bed.

Right now, let's decide together that we are going to be intentional with the aesthetic we desire for our houses. We will no longer default to a standard of comparison, but proactively look forward to the beauty and richness that already exists within our four walls. To do this, I invite you on an active journey to uncover what kind of you-shaped home you desire. Instead of looking around to determine your framework, I will lead you to first take a journey inward. Decide right now that your home's purpose is not its appearance but is related to your heart. When we make the heart of our home our plumb line, matching a standard of social media takes a back seat to what matters more.

Great designs begin with you.

Because great designs begin with you. Your wants. Your needs. Your family's priorities. Why would you want your home to look like an online designer's place? A space that parrots another's work may look beautiful, but it will never be functional or deeply connected to the growing needs of your household. Guess what? *You* get to choose the end result. There's no rule book to follow as you imagine the beauty of your home. You have my permission to evaluate your needs, add a hefty dose of fun, and craft the kind of home your family (no matter what shape it comes in) is wildly enthusiastic about entering.

After all, our homes are one of the biggest investments we will make. Home is the place where we might raise our kids, establish lifelong memories, and strengthen our relationships. The effort we spend making them lovely (to us!) is not in vain. I have spent my career helping people create unique homes because I believe when we reside in peaceful spaces with purpose, we can then naturally strengthen and invest in the people we love most.

FINDING THE HEART OF YOUR HOME

When we look to social media, magazines, and the latest renovation shows for design inspiration, messages swirl around us like noisy chatter. These voices interrupt our peace, hollering what we *should* want, who we *should* look like, and when we *should* reach these goals. These beautiful inspirational photos can create clutter and confusion. They cause us to forsake our own situations for the sake of pursuing an ideal that actually doesn't exist. I instantly am reminded of the time I was renovating on a tight budget and showed my contractor my example of a stunning kitchen to emulate. He laughed in my face. I found out later that it was Tom Brady and Giselle Butcher's home, a multimillion-dollar estate. The standard I hoped to emulate was not only out of my league but was far beyond what most of the world can afford. Yet it was online, so it became my expectation.

To achieve clarity, I invite you to do the opposite of the norm. First, turn off your phone to quiet the cacophony of the online space, then take stock of what resides in your heart. Have you ever considered that a beautiful home might consist of more than carefully curated furniture, art, and rugs? I contend the feel of a lovely space delves much deeper than the furniture choices, because a beautiful home has heart. Not just any heart—your heart.

The journey of finding the heart of my home felt more like trudging through quicksand. Those early years felt like a crash course from Mistake University, and I got an A for lessons learned. Have you noticed the first pancake you make on the griddle comes out a little wonky, not quite perfect? But with a little practice, your next try will be much nicer. Our first few houses can be like our first pancake. A lot of us go through the early years without a real design style. Calling dibs on discarded family items is more common than shopping new. In my early years of living in my own space, having a creative and resourceful eye came in handy as I furnished my starter home with hand-me-downs and items from garage sales. Somehow, I turned my meager "five loaves" of furniture castoffs into a home that looked inviting to others.

When my first baby arrived, there was already too much month at the end of the money. When I decided to stay home with our newborn, my family adjusted to our new, even tighter budget guidelines. But we were the proud beaming parents, ready to invite our elders into our humble home. On the day our relatives popped in to meet our days-old new bundle of joy, we were excited to show off what grown-ups we had become and to lead them through a home tour. However, as soon as my grandmother walked in the door, she took one look around the inexpensive yet curated decor and yelled to her son in the next room over, "I thought you said they were poor."

While this story has now made it into the annals of awkward and hilarious family history, at the time, being labeled "poor" in front of an audience of relatives felt excruciating. Just when we thought we had fooled everyone, Grandma called us out in front of our loved ones and our new baby. *Close your ears, little baby. Don't listen to Grandma, she lies.*

Now, after working with hundreds of people to design their personal spaces, I realize the early pain of decorating your first home is quite universal. Few people have unlimited funds and can write check after check for their decor needs. While budgets vary, seldom can my clients tackle their entire list in one round. So, learning to be scrappy and practical has proved a useful practice for myself and others. It's normal and acceptable to do things in phases. Thankfully, your budget does not have to slow you down. In a bonus chapter at the end of the book, I have given you some of my best tips for how to secondhand shop to generate an upscale design on a budget.

Thankfully, there is something more paramount, more significant, to your home than the retail value of your furnishings. The decor of your home is simply the backup vocalist to the real star of the show—the story of the home. This narrative can unfold with vintage secondhand items as well as high-end antiques. The meaning of your space has less to do with what is in the home—and what those things cost—and much more to do with *who* is in the home and what their story is.

> The decor of your home is simply the backup vocalist to the real star of the show—the story of the home.

You might be unsure of what your story is, much less how to tell it through decor choices. Not to worry, that is precisely what we will work through in our time together. First, I want you to consider a scenario.

What if I could give you a magic pill that promised higher self-esteem, greater academic competence, more advanced social competence, and fewer behavioral issues? This capsule would also provide the grit to face potential problems and help ward off bouts of anxiety and depression, resulting in an overall happier human. It sounds too good to be true, right? Not only would most people want this pill for themselves, but they would also likely take an extra dose for their loved ones. The good news is we have access to those very results. Though not in a gelatin gummy, we can achieve these goals by focusing on something just as available—our stories.[1]

The story of our families, our history, how we met our partners, what is important to us, and how we connect. Each and every family is teeming with tales, and research proves when we pass down our stories, we're actually giving our children all the benefits of the "magic pill," as well as teaching them hope and resilience.[2] Our words carry so much weight that when we speak, we give our loved ones the tools they will carry into the future, simply by allowing them to relate to where we have been. And just as we tell these stories with our words, we should also tell them in the details we use to furnish our homes, including tangible reminders of the history and heritage of our families.

To begin telling your story, let's first explore your home. What room do you feel conversation thrives in? Where does connection with others feel at its best?

These answers will vary depending on your space. Some people gather in the kitchen, crowding around the island while cooking or snacking. Others might converse around the dinner table, talking over each other as they pass plates of delicious foods. Some families have created an entire additional outdoor room on the porch, as simple as a semicircle of Adirondack chairs or as complex as a built-in kitchen with a mounted flatscreen TV. No matter where the social spot is in your home, you can find ideas for how to aid conversation through room flow sprinkled throughout this book.

As we begin to explore your story, please take note of the limitations in catch-all vocabulary. When I use the terms "home" or "family," please read that to be inclusive of family and home in *all* walks of life. A home or a family is not subject to the number of people who reside there. Unmarried people do not need to wait until they have a spouse, or reach some other external milestone, to create a home. They can create the essence of a comforting space now by embracing who they are, what their story is, and who they invest in as they grow community through their relationships. Home is reflected in multiple beautiful ways, and the definition of family is certainly not dictated by the number of people living under the same roof—or the way they're related. Some people choose to live with a chosen family of friends who, while not residing under their roof, are still a large part of their story. Let's redefine family and remember that it does not come in only one form but is as varied as everyone's favorite crayon box from kindergarten class—the oversized one with the built-in sharpener.

May I be your trusted guide as we uncover your home's story together? In the chapters to come, I will introduce you to the groundwork I walk clients through to build a foundation for a home that truly reflects their stories. Next, I'll show you examples to help you visualize how you can create *your* style in your space, room by room. I'll also offer specific, practical ideas of how to combine and utilize furniture arrangements that will translate to any location and style. Because I would rather show than tell, I will be weaving in real-life examples of what I have learned from my family of origin and how I have incorporated these lessons into living with my current family. Please do not be tempted to implement everything you learn immediately. These ideas will apply to you differently as the stages of your life and family evolve. I invite you to utilize the suggestions that fit your prevailing life stage, then make notes to revisit the rest later.

Finally, after your space feels right, I will guide you through the art of celebrating your people. Once you've intentionally created the story of your home, weaving love and beauty throughout, the reward is to share it with those you treasure most. By the end of this book, I want you to feel empowered that you have what it takes to make the best design choices for your home, as well as confident that you can tell an authentic story of your family—whatever that looks like for you.

Care to join me? Let's journey together to create the atmosphere you've been longing for. Hop in the passenger seat of this pink convertible and don your most glamorous Audrey Hepburn scarf and sunglasses. I have already packed the car so full that it overflows. Oversized parcels tied with large, loopy bows are bursting out of the back seat, scattered among smaller brown paper packages tied up with string, for the love of Julie Andrews. The exciting part is, if you look closely, you will see your name hand-lettered on all the gift tags. I uncovered the ample resources you already have and packed them with us—ready to place them in strategic locations to make maximum, joyful impact in your home. And like any good road trip, I made an epic playlist and brought snacks. So grab a drink, buckle up, and let's journey this road together.

ACTION STEPS
TO CREATE
A GREAT FIRST
IMPRESSION

When you enter a home for the first time, what is the first thing that grabs your attention?

The scent?

The furniture?

The layout of the house?

The smile of the person who answers the door?

Something else?

Next time you visit a new space, note the details that form your first impression. When I started paying more attention, I was surprised when what I thought I would notice first and what I actually observed were not the same. You also might observe new data about yourself when you take note of your impressions when you walk into an unfamiliar space. Or it could confirm the importance of what you already suspected.

Now consider what you learned or confirmed about yourself. How can you incorporate those observations in creating your desired first impression to your home?

HOW TO START YOUR STORY

What Is Your Decorating Style?

As my favorite governess said before she burst into song in *The Sound of Music*, "Let's start at the very beginning, a very good place to start."[1] Before we can start ABC-ing and Do-Re-Me-ing, we need to decide what story we want to tell. The transformative questions found on the Client Questionnaire (see the next page) are not to be skimmed over quickly. I think of this section like a pastry chef making their famous dough from scratch. Kneading it, pounding it, turning it over only to turn it over again. They don't give up until it is the exact consistency to rise and bake into the quality of bread they can take pride in.

Ruminate on these questions. Even better, take them to a place where peace comes easy and a deep breath feels natural. As you feel the quiet take hold of you and hear the scurry of your mind begin to settle, formulate your answers. This foundation is not to be rushed but savored. The more details you can draw out, the more material will be present to inform your story. Grab your favorite journal and brainstorm every detail you can think of. Nothing is too small to leave out.

What rises to the surface might just surprise you.

CLIENT QUESTIONNAIRE

What is your design vibe?

When we begin to dream of what story we want to tell in our home, an effective place to start is where our story began—our childhood home. Once we begin to observe the story that was told, we learn more about if we want to continue the same story or tell a new one.

- Think of a time when you felt at home growing up. What was going on? This could be centered around a happy memory, a certain location, or the feeling you got when you listened to a special new song for the first time. The sense of home comes in many forms. Whatever speaks "home" to you is the right answer.
- Growing up, what did you love about your home?
- What did you want to change about your childhood home? What would you change about it now, looking back on it? Are those things the same?
- What objects in your current home bring you joy?
- If your house caught on fire, what would you save?
- Where do you feel stuck in your space now?
- What has kept you from processing forward?
- How do you want your home to feel? What emotions do you want it to invoke? How do you want people to feel when they leave your space?

ONE

BELONGING STORY
The Living Room

CONGRATULATIONS TO ME! I bought a historic home.

This new investment stands at over one hundred years old, is in need of renovation, and is painted a garish pastel assortment of last year's Easter eggs. If you owned such a home, which of the tasks below would you tackle first upon moving?

A. Unpacking boxes

B. Arranging furniture

C. Painting walls

D. Touring your home in front of an audience of millions on national TV

If you had asked me what I would be doing two months after moving into my new home, you can probably guess what the most unlikely option would have been. Yet, as I sat in front of the bright lights of the camera, with my watch ticking toward midnight, a film crew surrounded me, and our night's end was not in sight.

Candidly, at the adventure's outset, I was not clear about what I had volunteered to do. I simply responded to an email that asked, "Do you live in the Dallas area and love your home?" I did, indeed, love the charm of the historic house I had just moved to, with its wraparound porch and gingerbread trim. I saw past the excessive rainbow paint to the potential it could have, and I knew the first step was a massive paint job. In a bingo game of candy-colored wall paint, my bingo marker would stay busy.

Primary bedroom—lavender.

Dining room—hot pink.

Guest bedroom—teal.

Outside—yellow, pink, and blue.

Bingo!

My first step was to overhaul the entire paint palette of the home, then I could begin general upkeep and neglected repairs. It was a huge undertaking, but thankfully, I had plenty of time to get things in order.

Today, in my current interior design role, I congratulate my clients when they reach the stage of buying their first piece of "grown-up" furniture. I call it furniture graduation. This is the special rite of passage when they use their hard-earned money to purchase a piece they love instead of the most recent family hand-me-down. When you're established enough to attain that first piece of furniture without having to suffer through a year's worth of ramen dinners first, go ahead and move over that tassel.

During this particular move, I had yet to receive my furniture diploma. This early home was a bit of a mishmash—definitely one of my first "pancakes." Yet despite secondhand decor, visitors still complimented the home, and most importantly, my family enjoyed it. After stretching a tight budget for years, I never considered feeling ashamed of making the best of what I had been given.

When I received a response back from the inquiry email, I learned that a national cable network was launching a traveling series in which four homeowners would tour and critique each other's homes, and the network was pleased to inform me of my progression through the first round of cuts for the Dallas episode. This would be shortly followed by another Skype call, then if I advanced, I'd have a phone call with the producer before being cast on the show.

After a whirlwind week of maintaining good hair and fresh lipstick for video interviews, I received the mind-boggling call that I had been chosen. I was cast as one of the four homeowners who would be featured on the episode of the new show! Ecstatic, I frantically ran around my house, celebrating like Kevin from *Home Alone* when he first realized he had the house to himself, then collapsed like an exhausted toddler who missed their nap.

After my initial elation, trepidation crept in. I knew the house was far from camera ready. We had just moved our family and had hardly unpacked. I did not know much about TV filming schedules but reasoned that since movies took years to film, TV must also move slowly, and I would have plenty of time to update the crucial spaces. However, when they released the filming schedule, my hope sank as I learned that the entire network filming crew would arrive on my doorstep in two weeks. Two weeks?! I had barely lived in this town, much less this house, and now I had invited a camera crew over? My lamenting was cut short because I had to organize my pantry. I wasn't sure if the episode tour would include the pantry, but mine was going to shine—right after I swept away the dust bunnies under my bed.

There is much more to creating a home than making it beautiful.

The first day of filming confirmed my growing internal fear. The other three houses on the show looked like mansions to me. I knew they were valued at least four times the price of my humble home. I felt way in over my head. *Why did they even choose me?* I pondered. I *thought* I loved my house until I began comparing it to others. As I began to see my home through new eyes, my eclectic style seemed jumbled, and what once looked artfully distressed now just seemed threadbare. The other houses on the episode had more stuff, better stuff, and stuff I wanted but honestly could not afford. Dread soon topped off this discontentment cocktail. Not only would I see how I compared to the other homes—the premise of the show—but a national audience would watch along with me. I was petrified of falling short in front of everyone. This exciting event somehow turned into another instance of "*I thought you said they were poor,*" but this time all my friends were watching.

After a week of confidential filming, I signed paperwork promising everything but my left kidney to not discuss anything that occurred. The contestants were even prohibited from talking about their experiences with each other, which meant the first time I heard any feedback about my home was when the show broadcast on TV.

In the weeks leading up to the air date, anxiety spread in my spirit like the flu. My thoughts ping-ponged between despair and optimism. Was this my breakout design debut and the next step toward Reese Witherspoon hiring me? (Because, let's face it, once she met me, we would obviously become best friends.) Or would my best attempts to furnish a home be laughable and my shortcomings paraded in a public forum? Did an in-between exist?

My friends reached out with invitations to watch parties, but I could hardly leave my house. I hunkered down with family members, inhaling Tums like breath mints. When airtime finally came, I squeezed on the couch between my mom and my sister, flipped on the TV, and got ready to bare my soul.

SITTING ON THAT COUCH, feeling so much self-doubt, I never would have guessed that people would one day ask for my input on their design style. Uncertainty of our design skills in our own homes is a legitimate feeling, and my hope is to help you strengthen those design muscles and bolster your confidence by giving you practical applications to implement design ideas. Oddly enough, I don't even see myself as a typical designer. After all, some interior designers might clutch their pearls to hear me say I believe there is much more to creating a home than making it beautiful. Of course, we want it to look amazing. But we also want it to feel amazing. Each person deserves a peaceful respite where you can walk through the door, relax your shoulders, unclench your jaw, and think, *It feels so good to be home.* That is what a beautiful home means to me.

YOUR BELONGING SPACE

As we build the foundation of the home that tells your story and the story of your family, let's start with the room designed for hanging out—the living room. Living rooms are the common areas of the home and can be made up of every distinctive architectural shape and configuration imaginable. Though the layout of our homes will vary vastly, the purpose will be aligned—they are the gathering places. For me this feels like:

- a respite away from the hurried world
- the space I walk into and my shoulders instantly relax
- the spot where the high anxiety I carry feels manageable
- the place I can sink into the sofa and prop my feet up and feel the comfort and peace around me
- the livable area where I don't have to stress if the water spills on the hardwoods or the dog lies on the rug
- the site where I connect with others through rich conversation and spend time with family and friends

I encourage you not to approach your home like a showplace or a museum. If I am a guest in a new home and I am preoccupied with guarding small kids from untouchables or breaking unspoken house rules, connection does not come easy. In fact, I'm likely too on edge to have the margin to engage with anyone on a deeper level. By the visit's end, I am so exhausted I usually want to go home where I can relax. In these cases, priorities are flip-flopped and the home design is elevated above the people in it. That is not the feeling I want to create for my visitors. How about you? What story do you want your living room to tell?

When I hunted for kitchen countertops for my last home, I longed for the gauzy veining of Carrera Marble but hesitated purchasing it because of its reputation for being high maintenance. (I imagine if Carrera Marble joined a high school clique, it would be the deeply emotional one that opted out of frog dissection by citing animal cruelty and writing a protest

The invitation to "come as you are" is more than Nirvana lyrics.

letter to the principal.) It is sensitive. Thus, many contractors will steer you away because it can "etch" if an acidic substance spills on it, and it shows imperfections plainly. My best friend had recently installed this marble in her kitchen, so I consulted her for advice.

"We have decided that we will embrace the limitations of marble," she told me. "I am fine if it etches because it is part of the character. I am not going to live my life worrying about my kitchen countertop."

This healthy outlook empowered me with newfound freedom. I moved forward with the Carrera Marble, loved the look, and hardly noticed when imperfections appeared. Once I had the framework determined for who served who, the marble was relegated to its rightful place. Like an independent five-year-old stomping my foot, I will declare that my marble—or anything else about my home—is not the boss of me.

Consider your home. Is an unwritten standard for beauty creating a disconnect when you have guests? If so, would you rather your home be lived-in or enjoyed from afar? Your answer will dictate the essence of the home you hope to create.

In one of my favorite business books, *The 7 Habits of Highly Effective People*, author Stephen Covey teaches the powerful practice of beginning "with the end in mind."[1] While his intended purpose is not home-related, his methodology can be usefully applied to our end goal. For instance, as I brainstormed content for this book, I imagined my desired outcome for my readers upon turning the last page. I envisioned you would close the cover, filled with new boldness, and you would start applying what you learned by confidently tackling a problem area in your home. I decided the goal for this book is to empower people to create a space that tells the story of their family. I long to grow their confidence as they surround themselves with things they love, giving less thought to design rules and focusing more intentionally on connection.

I want to invite you to do the same practice as we consider your living room. Let us begin with the end in mind. Imagine what you want this common area to be. Allow yourself to dream as you consider how your family will spend a Friday night or what a guest's impression will be after they walk out the door. If the president of your local social club paid you a surprise visit, what kind of atmosphere would you want them to happen upon? What would they see? Do you envision your loved ones piled on the couch to watch movies together? If so, I foresee decor choices like plush, cozy couches and ottomans and a large TV to gather around. Would you rather create an intimate place for one-on-one conversations? In that case, this might be better accomplished by having small armchairs scattered around the room in pairs.

My desire for your living room is that it becomes the "belonging space." What's more, I see this belonging space as a room where the invitation to "come as you are" is more than Nirvana lyrics. I envision your living room transformed into a shelter from the world, where folks are expected to be themselves, where authenticity and truth-telling hold value. It's a spot where the movie night uniform is pajama pants, and removing makeup after a long day is the only prerequisite to propping your feet up on the coffee table and enjoying a sweet tea. Doesn't that sound like a home you want to live in? It does for me.

Now, what practical actions can we take to create that feeling? First of all, don't allow this space to get too precious. This might mean this area holds an open invitation to kids and pets. Everything in view is allowed to be touched or examined. After all, the living room hosts the most traffic in the house. If your home were AwesomeTown, USA, your living room would be on Main Street. So if a keepsake requires instructions to handle with care or not be handled at all, it is preferable to keep it in a more private area. When my youngest son was small, we visited a home that kept free weights on the living room shelves. It was like a tractor beam when my toddler would get them in view—he could see nothing else. But each time he drew near, he was chastised for picking them up. Once we stored them out of sight, the temptation was easily avoided. Lesson: Do not make things weird. Avoid putting your guests in an awkward situation by putting any untouchables behind closed doors.

Conversely, while formal, unlivable areas do not aid in connection and gathering, neither does chaos. While the living room is the main thoroughfare, I don't suggest it turn into a catch-all. Is the room cluttered? Is there too much furniture filling the space? Are you keeping an item you don't need or want out of a sense of duty? That last one is a very common affliction and is typically caused by two reasons.

1. It belonged to Grandma—Oh, Grandma. We love you so much. We just do not love your china cabinet because, honestly, it is ugly.

Many people struggle with unwanted hand-me-down furniture and keep it out of obligation, because they believe it somehow honors their loved one's memory. They do not like this piece. It is not an heirloom or even attractive, but Granny got it at the local Furniture Mart and they think if they don't keep it in their home, it will not honor her life. This unattractive piece has become a shackle that does not fit the aesthetic of the room, but to discard it would bring guilt. Before I unpack why *all* of these things are untrue, let me list the second reason people often keep things they dislike.

2. The initial investment was significant to their budget—This is really the opposite side of the same coin. The thought is, *I do not like this anymore, but I paid $XXX for it, so we have to keep it*. The high price tag prohibits them from discarding the piece they no longer currently use or enjoy.

We only have one home. One space to create our story. I contend that every item that surrounds us is something that needs to, as Marie Kondo would say, "spark joy." When we allow obligation or guilt to dictate our surroundings, we are no longer the bosses of our homes. They no longer serve us. We become a subordinate to these items, carting them around from house to house, perhaps adding a coat of paint to them in an attempt to make them look fresh. If you would not buy an item again, do not keep it now. As we discussed earlier, furniture is not a financial investment—it is a personal one. If you bought a pricey piece of furniture that served you well, you got your money's worth. If you kept it for many years, you got more than your money's worth.

I, Courtney Warren, give you my official designer's permission to let it go.

Does it really honor your loved one to keep an antiquated piece of furniture that you do not want or like? Unless Grandma literally gave you a deathbed utterance—"Make sure my bedside table carries on the family name"—an educated guess tells me she did not care one bit about that china cabinet. But she probably *would* care about your happiness. In later chapters we will discuss more meaningful ways to honor a relative through design that will actually enhance your space, not distract from it. Allow yourself to have peace and pay this item forward to someone who needs it more than you do.

(Note to my boys: Don't feel obligated to keep any of my stuff. Please sell it and pay for the therapy I am sure you will need. After all, when you were too small to be out of sight, I made you go in the ladies' room with me, even after you each repeatedly told me, "I AM NOT A GRILL" because that is how you said girl and it was too cute to correct.)

For all the variety our living rooms may have, a few crucial decisions aid our goals of connection. To recap:

- Let your home serve you, not the other way around.
- Strike a balance between chaotic and unapproachable.
- Get rid of the piece that prohibits the room from feeling fresh.
- If you would not buy it again, don't keep it.

THINGS TO CONSIDER
BEFORE YOU MOVE FURNITURE

We have brainstormed what story we want to tell in our living room and discussed ways to balance a beautiful room while still making it practical for real-life factors, like kids and pets. Now let's get practical and discuss how to arrange the living room in a way that tells your story.

 An inviting space for those who reside there

Practical Applications:

- *Choose a comfy couch with plenty of seating for everyone.* Don't create a musical chairs game when it's time to relax. If I have six people in my family, I have more than six places to sit.
- *Display photos of loved ones in the room.* This small gesture not only reminds our dearest of the wonderful memories we have made together but also confirms their importance in our lives.
- *Thoughtfully examine your needs before purchasing.* I consider the relaxation styles of my family to determine what will work best in the spaces we inhabit. A client of mine had three teenage sons, and once we began our design work, we realized his space needed chaises or a sectional. When these boys relaxed, they *lounged*, stretching themselves out as far as they could—arms and legs so splayed out that a typical couch would not hold them all. By considering the entire room and how his family might use it, we were able to make an informed purchase that would serve their needs and last longer.

A place where visitors will feel welcome and comfortable

Practical Applications:

- *Provide hospitality in the entry of your home.* In designing an entry, I like to consider the Hawaiian custom of greeting someone with a flower lei upon arrival. Obviously it might get awkward if you crown guests with fresh flowers when they walk through the front door, but I do want you to consider the spirit of the welcoming gesture. Like the tradition of offering leis to guests, how can you set the tone of a lovely visit? The following ideas are things I've noticed when I entered someone's home.

- *Make a peaceful first impression.* Minimize the chaos of your home and allow the visitor to enter peacefully. This means putting energetic pets in another area when guests first arrive. Even if they say they adore dogs, a jumping ball of fur inadvertently scratching them is hardly a peaceful welcome and most people are too courteous to say any differently. The onus is on the homeowner to anticipate needs and make guests feel comfortable upon arrival. Remove the overzealous animals and allow the first impression to be one of peace.

- *Offer guests a beverage when they arrive.* Ensure side tables are stationed throughout the room for guests to rest their drinks on while they sit. These tables should be positioned an arm's length from each seat for easy access.

- *Store extra toiletries on hand in case someone finds they need a place to stay.* You never know when a long visit might lead to an impromptu slumber party. While not directly needed in the living room, the extra hospitality of having toiletries available for them in a pinch can make a guest feel valued and allows for spontaneity.

A comfortable space that balances form and function

Practical Applications:

- *Keep throws and blankets handy.* Perhaps these can be slung over the backs of chairs and couches, for everyone to use and curl up in.
- *Ensure every seat in the room has an unobstructed view of the TV.* This means most of the seating faces the TV and is not blocked by other furniture.
- *Invite folks to put their feet up.* Scatter ottomans or coffee tables about the room as a way to encourage folks to feel comfortable. No item in the space should be too precious to be interacted with.
- *Safeguard all items on a child's level.* Confirm no injury or item-breaking will occur if handled by a child.
- *Utilize table lamps to soften harsh overhead light.* Accent lighting provides a warmer glow that overhead lights cannot mimic.
- *Employ curtains or blinds in front of windows when darkness is beneficial.* This can reduce a glare when watching TV or when you need privacy at night. But because I prefer natural light, I keep my windows unobstructed throughout the day to flood the room with sunshine.

 A well-thought-out atmosphere where relationships are strengthened

Practical Applications:

- *Resist placing furniture along the wall, unless it is a very small room.* In a large room, lining up furniture along the wall hinders conversations since it seats people too far away from each other.
- *Allow natural sitting areas to aid in better discussions.* Let these sitting areas take shape by arranging chairs a few feet apart. If you

follow the advice above, arrange furniture in the middle of the room and anchor it with a sofa table behind the couch.

- *Add a rug to make the room warmer and more inviting.* A rug helps add texture and color to a room and separates the sitting area from the other areas. It also breaks up the seemingly miles of flooring and provides variation when there is a lot of wood, tile, or carpet.

- *Break up an oversized room by creating several sitting areas.* Set up several smaller sitting areas throughout the room, perhaps placing one on one end and mirroring it on the opposite side. By creating smaller sitting areas, a large room feels more intimate and people can more easily connect. Rugs can also act as MVPs by creating a perimeter to help define the room.

- *Allow patterns to complement, not compete.* Decide on a focal point, then plan everything else accordingly. If you want your rug to be a focal piece, pick a more subtle sofa pattern and a bolder rug. If you love the bright design of the sofa, an understated, solid rug or curtain with similar tones to each other would pair well.

 A space where all the senses are indulged, when possible

Practical Applications:

- *Play soft music in the background.* Keep it at a low volume so it can easily be spoken over. If things get too noisy, mute it to encourage conversation to be continued.

- *Burn a candle or diffuse essential oils.* Scents are a soothing way to create a peaceful space.

- *Pitch the threadbare throw and choose a velvety replacement.* You know the one I mean. It's the blanket that makes your feet cold because your toe sticks out of the big hole in the bottom. Time to toss it.

- *Have your visitors' or family members' favorite snacks on hand.* Keep a candy bowl or fruit plate out. If you don't know their preferences, chocolates are a tried-and-true favorite, or a mix of fruit and nuts.
- *Consider whether a living room TV is a priority for your lifestyle.* I have designed our various living room spaces both with and without a TV, and they have all worked well for that particular season and space. Remember, this space should serve you and those you love. Abandon whatever expectations you've been self-imposing. You have permission to break them.

 ## A completed home that features beloved items

Practical Applications:

- *Purchase or upcycle pieces that you truly enjoy.* If budget constraints slow the process of completing a room, consider buying secondhand.
- *Edit the home.* Remove anything you would not buy again. Have a garage sale. Donate unwanted items to your favorite charity. Put them out on the curb. Post on Facebook Marketplace. Paul Simon sang, "There are fifty ways to leave your lover,"[2] and I am saying there are fifty-one ways to clear your clutter. As long as you have low expectations for recouping the investment, any way will work.
- *Regulate impulse buys.* When I'm at HomeGoods and tempted to fill my cart with new, adorable items I love but I do not need, I resist the urge to impulse buy and, instead, I rely on the stop and snap. Meaning I stop and snap a photo of it instead. If I am still pining after it like a middle school crush a day or two later, I know it is a solid purchase. However, if it is not worth the trouble of returning to the store—let's be honest, if it is not worth putting on my makeup— I just saved money and probably some attic space by regulating an impulse buy.

STEPS TO CREATE YOUR ROOM

You're ready now, I can feel it. It's "go-time." The real progress starts when you start applying your new knowledge to your real life. If you feel stuck, here are the simple steps I use to "tune up" a room. Which is convenient, because they actually spell the word TUNE.

THINK   UPDATE   NOTICE   EXECUTE

First, take some time to **THINK** about the hopes you have for this space.

- How can you best tell the story of your family in your living room?
- How do you want them to feel as they spend time in that room?
- Does the flow of the furniture lend itself to your objective? If you want to encourage conversation, do the chairs sit close enough to each other? Is one sofa on the opposite side of the room from the other so you have to yell to hear each other?

Use common sense and observation to evaluate what is working and what is not. If you want input as you brainstorm, ask your family. If they are anything like mine, they will love to give their opinions.

After you've spent time thinking about your goals for the space, make necessary **UPDATEs** to bring about the needed improvements. This might mean moving chairs closer together or adding tables for drinks. Once your room is arranged, **NOTICE** the way people interact with the space and make notes as you go. Are additional updates needed? Keep your eye out for any issues that may arise with your new layout and then make a plan to **EXECUTE** changes. For instance, if viewers on one side of the room repeatedly ask you to increase the volume on the TV, perhaps the speakers need to be adjusted or the chairs need to be moved closer to the speakers. If you really listen, people will tell you what they need. Go through the "tuning" process as many times as needed. The checklist is complete when the space meets your original desires. Now, look at you. You did it. You finished your first room.

BACK TO THE COUCH and the anxiety I felt as I awaited my home's debut on TV. As the episode began, my jittery nerves eased. When left on cruise control, my personality shifts between playful and personable, and the producers captured it, as well as a couple of funny quips. Since my love language is a captive audience that laughs at my jokes, the foreboding pressure on my shoulders began to release. I even started to laugh at myself upon hearing my Texas drawl through the TV. (Does anyone enjoy hearing a recording of themselves?) In the episode, I walked through one home and stumbled upon an enormous full-size stuffed grizzly bear on its hind legs. I was taken off guard by this unexpected, furry giant and yelled, "I think I saw a bear." Only, with my Southern accent, it sounded as if I energetically exclaimed, "I THANK I saw a BEER!" I didn't live that down for a while after airing. People randomly yelled that phrase at me in public for months following.

As promising as things seemed at the start of the episode, they still hadn't gotten to my property yet. Finally, my stomach flipped over as the segment containing my house began. What would the other contestants think of my home? Would the critique be gentle or brutal?

My self-consciousness oozed into humiliation when they critiqued my style. One contestant spoke to the camera with disdain, saying that I did not have a single piece of art in my entire house, only family photos.

Now, over a decade later, I remember that young, scared version of me watching the show with horror, and I'm flooded with empathy. If I could speak to her, I would sit on that couch and tell her that risks take courage, especially in such a personal matter. I would reassure her that other young mothers rarely have art collections and that choice of prioritizing photography was unrelated to inferiority or bumpkin status. Most of all, I would applaud her sincere attempt to decorate a beautiful, warm, inviting home on a budget and reassure her that she had plenty of time to hone her skill. I would reveal that the perceived negativity was actually productive and created a turning point for her career. Then I would feel awkward speaking to myself in the third person.

Because, as humble as my first attempt at designing a home appeared to some, it still resonated with others. Those people liked my style and wanted to re-create it in their homes. I allowed the feedback I received to sharpen my skills, while still acknowledging that the opinion of one person was simply that, an opinion. It is just like the nursery rhyme says. Sticks and stones may break my bones and TV shows will not dictate my value or worth.

My experience taught me this—*your home is built for you*. You get to choose what you want to include and leave out. Using fundamental design tips as guideposts will ensure a better outcome, but ultimately, your home is there to serve you. If you want to use all family photos instead of art, that is a good choice—for *you*.

Surrounding yourself with things that you love and that bring you joy is more meaningful than keeping up with an expectation or design rule.

ACTION STEPS

TO CREATE YOUR LIVING ROOM STORY

We discussed numerous ideas on how to tell your story through the design of your living room. Now that you are familiar with the concept, I invite you to consider your home now. Below are questions that will assist in helping you brainstorm what is working and what you would like to improve. The answers to these questions will create an action plan to help you better tell your story through your design.

- Is the way your living room is set up currently serving those who live there? Why or why not?
- What works in your home?
- What is your favorite part about this space?
- What is currently telling your family's story?
- What is your least favorite part about the room?

- Is there a small change you can make without much effort to improve your satisfaction? What is it?
- What big change would help improve your satisfaction?
- What one step can you take today that would get you closer to accomplishing the big step listed? Is it possible?
- What do you aspire for this room to be? How do you want it to feel? If you had to describe it in one word, what would that word be? If you could use two, what would the second word be?
- What can you do now to bring that about?
- What would you need to put off until a later time to bring about that change?
- What action would help you know if your changes are effective?

Once your desired changes are implemented, use your answers to make changes and then evaluate their efficacy. If things are not quite right the first time, cycle through the steps until they are. Once you have created a space you are satisfied with, feel proud and accomplished that you did it! High-five!

This living room truly didn't involve many changes, despite the drastic transformation. The original incarnation was dated, dirty, and drab. The ho-hum wallpaper and peach paint likely covered years of bad decorating decisions. The original paneling gave the room a portable building vibe, but a fresh coat of paint presented it more like shiplap. Replacing the dingy blue carpet with hardwood flooring and removing the popcorn texture from the ceiling made this design look decades fresher. I wanted to highlight the vaulted ceiling, so we added a bit of molding to replicate an architectural feature. Finally, replacing the light fixture and adding a seating area turned this eyesore into a stunning, airy space ready for entertaining.

feature

STYLESENSE DESIGN QUIZ

What Sense Will Complement Your Story?

Design is primarily assumed to be a visual medium and for good reason. After all, what our eyes take in often plays a crucial role in the room. We process color that mixes with patterns and informs how a space looks. But what we may not realize is that our other senses are just as crucial in creating an aesthetic. Just as body language trumps verbal communication, the entire feeling of a space is much more important than what can be seen only with the naked eye. In fact, it's nearly impossible to separate the senses from each other. Don't believe me? Put it to the test. Eat a piece of chocolate and try to imagine what it would taste like if you could not smell it.

In a corporate setting, an effective designer will consider how to balance a noisy collaborative workspace with a quiet zone or how far to distance the trash chute from the cafeteria. Each space is designed with other factors in mind. Likewise, we need to consider how our senses can be used to complement each other in our homes. If you are like me and have been asleep since kindergarten class when they taught the five senses, they are sight, hearing, smell, taste, and touch.

I would like to introduce you to Style-Sense, a tool to assist you as you determine which sense is most important to enhance in your space and how to include all senses as you tell your story.

Of the five options, what sense do you most align with? Are you drawn to spaces that focus on one sense over others? What are some ways to incorporate some of the senses in your space? Are you utilizing all the senses in the design of your home?

Take this questionnaire to find out what your primary StyleSense is and learn how to use it to complement the story you tell in your space.

1. When you walk into a room, what's the first thing you notice?
    A. The onions simmering on the stove
    B. The temperature of the room
    C. Lamps or big windows that allow natural light in
    D. The dining settings on the table
    E. A space for quiet conversations

2. Think of a time when you felt uncomfortable in a space. Which of the following bothered you the most?
    A. A mysterious odor
    B. The air was too warm or too cold
    C. The use of harsh lighting
    D. Absence of options for food and drink
    E. The use of bold and busy colors

3. Which of the following chores do you tend to prioritize?
    A. Cleaning everything
    B. Vacuuming carpet
    C. Painting and decorating
    D. Arranging the kitchen
    E. Setting up the TV and sound system

4. Your bedroom has to have:

   A. Linen spray

   B. A plush blanket

   C. A wall painted in a color that makes a statement

   D. A glass of water on the nightstand

   E. A noise machine

5. When you do spring cleaning, what do you start with?

   A. Disinfecting everything

   B. Dusting

   C. Decluttering paperwork—old bills, papers, etc.

   D. Organizing the refrigerator and pantry

   E. Fixing squeaky doors

6. When you are sick, what comforts you?

   A. Essential oils

   B. A heating pad

   C. A dark room

   D. Chicken soup

   E. Complete silence

7. Which of the following is a must in your dream home?

   A. A garden with fresh flowers

   B. Soft rugs or carpets

   C. A wall of windows

   D. Fresh lemonade set out on the porch

   E. A quiet location away from a road

Now tally your answers. Note how many times you chose each letter. Is there a clear winner?

Did you choose mostly As? Consider incorporating more scents into your space.

Our sense of smell is a major player in the feeling of a space and is often overlooked. Scents are mostly linked to memories. The minute I walk into a gymnasium, my mind flashes to my elementary school PE class. Think about when you walk into someone else's home. Can you tell that they just burned salmon or cooked broccoli? Ick. Or does the home smell musty and, as a result, feel dingy? Perhaps the mix of aromas smells warm and inviting? There is a reason why realtors advise sellers to bake cookies if they want to sell their house quickly. Aromas make a difference. Likewise, luxe hotels pipe tasteful fragrances into the air to create a well-rounded experience. To incorporate our olfactory sense into your design, utilize candles, diffusers, and sprays. Peppermint, lemon, citrus, and eucalyptus are some of my favorites. Each scent is said to be tied to different emotions. Fresh flowers, fruit, and plants can mix well to provide a clean or fragrant aroma. To re-create the zen hotel experience at home, dab essential oil inside a toilet paper roll before putting it on the holder, or soak a cotton ball in a fragrant oil and place it underneath the trash bag. You will be surprised how pleasant the result is.

Did you choose mostly Bs? Consider incorporating more tactile sensations into your space.

Textures, surfaces, and materials are combined to create a feeling—good or bad—in a home. How would you describe a kitchen with long, slick countertops and bright white lights? Most people would say it feels sterile. Now, contrast that feeling with a cottage living room, with soft sofas, fuzzy throw blankets, and a plush rug underneath your bare feet. You might say that space feels cozy. Notice I described the textures of the room, and the result was a feeling.

Temperature can also aid in your response to a room. Some people do not utilize the AC in the summer, and some turn it down to 68 degrees. Upon opening the front door, the rush of air in those spaces will feel very different.

Consider the textures of your sofa, bed, or comforter. How do your sheets feel? Are they pilled with little balls from wear and washing? What does not feel soft anymore? It might be time to invest in some new items that are soothing to the touch.

Did you choose mostly Cs? Consider how you've incorporated visual elements into your design style and bring them into focus.

Visual elements are the most obvious factor of design, but the effects of visual mediums are not as well known. We can use factors such as color to invoke an internal response. Color is proven to impact mood and feeling. Businesses spend many marketing dollars and hours of research groups to determine brand colors that suggest the feeling they hope to invoke when people use their service. In the same manner, color in your home can invoke the emotion that you are striving to create. Blue suggests peace. Red, on the other hand, is used for strong emotions. A color wheel will give the specifics for every shade and can be a helpful tool to consult as you brainstorm what hues to use. Patterns, fabrics, colors, lighting, and textures—they all combine to create an aesthetically pleasing space.

Did you choose mostly Ds? Consider incorporating more taste into your space.

Clearly, utilizing taste in design is not literal. Rather, it can be interpreted through the way the space is set up to incorporate savoring food and drink. One of the most common offenders I see is a sitting area without any tables to house a drink.

Ideas that incorporate taste in the space include a coffee bar or mini refrigerator in the home office. Perhaps there is a small bowl of mints by the entry doorway or a bottle of water nestled in a snack basket left in a guest room. After all, there is something about the minute you walk through someone's doorway that universally makes you want to eat their food. Or is that just me?

Did you choose mostly Es? Consider what your space sounds like.

In college I lived in a loft with upstairs neighbors who used rolling chairs to play hockey. You can probably guess that living beneath them was a loud, roll-y sound explosion that was fun for only the hockey players. Do you live near a noisy road or train? Do you have neighbors who can hear you through paper-thin walls and vice versa? Do your floorboards creak or does your HVAC shutter when it turns on? All of these contribute to the sound of your home. To create the background noise you want and combat those you do not, grab a sound machine or a fan as a good starting place. Perhaps having a speaker system or surround sound playing your favorite music would be a nice addition, or even a vintage-looking radio with Bluetooth capabilities.

While this quiz focuses on the sense that speaks most powerfully to you, take note of the other answers as well. They will act as a guide to follow as you create the story of your home. Allow the results to prime your mind to consider what senses are invoked when you visit a space. Choose your favorite ideas from each category and incorporate them in a way that most resonates with you. This will allow the senses to tag team and work how they work best—by collaborating and weaving together to create a powerful story.

TWO

BUILDING STORY

The Kitchen

WHEN MY FAMILY GATHERS, we do it in the kitchen. We live by the first half of the Blue Bell ice cream motto: "We eat all we can and sell the rest." In the Olympics of loving great food, we would place on the podium. After all, anytime a stove fires up, the family crowds around to snack, because—much like our canine companions sniffing underfoot—we all know that food will eventually appear.

One Christmas Eve when I was a kid, after walking through the door following the candlelight service, I plopped down on the couch as my mom prepared dinner. From my angle, I watched as she closely examined the homemade chocolate cake on the counter. When we had left for church, the dessert had been freshly frosted and left to cool. Now, where fudge icing once overflowed, the cake sat scraped clean, almost like it had never been frosted at all.

"Did you scrape the frosting off this cake?" she wondered out loud.

I frowned. "No, that would be weird. Why would I do that?"

"I am not sure," she answered, almost to herself.

Incredulous, we could not figure out what happened. Why would a once-frosted cake now appear completely bare? We started questioning family members, all to no avail. The Christmas Kitchen Mystery of 1991 had commenced.

AS A MOM, I fondly recollect silly childhood stories and long to forge new ones with my growing boys. Parenting two boys as a girly girl occasionally feels like I'm summitting Boy Mountain in high heels with a handbag on my arm. I have not gotten my boy mom badge yet, but I will not stop until I do. I once heard a parenting expert say that the most effective method to encourage a teenager to talk is to engage them when they don't have to make eye contact—aka, in the car. This makes sense to me. What kid wants to gaze into their mom's eyes and bare their soul, perhaps while she awkwardly caresses their hand? This expert reasoned that when the young person is doing something else, the pressure subsides and sharing seems more approachable. As I have attempted this method, I've discovered the kitchen is another prime place to get those hands working and perhaps get a mouth moving. By assigning a responsibility and working alongside each other to accomplish a common goal, my kids and I connect in simple ways that we otherwise wouldn't. Moments spent cooking, stirring and chopping, sharing the countertop, and sharing a table together have become a strong base to cement lasting foundations. I believe the kitchen is a place to build and connect with family members over a common goal. It is the place where roots are formed and built upon, a building space for relationships.

Time spent in the kitchen stirs up nostalgia for many of us. Maybe your family gathering times, like mine, came with a side menu, and certain dishes were reserved for specific holidays. We heaped Seven Layer Salad on our plates once a year—only on Christmas Eve. In a clear, footed bowl, we stacked iceberg lettuce, bacon, peas, cheese, and salad dressing, all layered more meticulously than a J.Crew catalog model. As if we all agreed

The kitchen is a place to build and connect with family members over a common goal.

to an unspoken covenant, no one ever requested the same dish until 365 days later on the next Christmas Eve. It's as if the family was convinced this cold concoction held the magic that powers Santa's sleigh, so as responsible citizens it was our obligation to keep the Seven Layer Salad on the menu. It was not only this side but many other delicious dishes that consistently showed up like faithful friends, painstakingly produced by hands that demonstrated care and commitment through the various steps of putting together these creations. These trusted traditions felt like life pillars growing up, pinning a sometimes-uncertain childhood to reliable and consistent markers.

When my granny Helen expressed her deep love for me, it was through a skillet. Frozen pizza and dinosaur-shaped chicken nuggets? No way. When making French fries, my old-school granny peeled and cut the potatoes by hand, then fried them over the stove in piping-hot oil. Those crispy home-made offerings would rival any gourmet side at a high-end steakhouse.

Granny didn't mess around with pithy details such as calorie counts. Her hot buttered toast is folklore in our family, and only after attempting it as an adult did I realize how much butter is required to achieve the golden, warm toast. If she had four sticks of butter, she could make four pieces of toast. My mouth still waters at the thought of Granny's homemade dishes.

Every morning Granny opened her home to her neighbor Maggie to converse over coffee. They sat at the kitchen table with their steaming porcelain mugs and chatted about their latest health ailment or speculated on the current soap opera saga. I yearned to sit with them, always hankering to be one of the grown-ups. (I also ached to impart my juicy soap opera observations because I knew that Marlena's evil twin did not really have amnesia—she was totally faking it!)

When I tentatively requested to join them the first time, Granny thoughtfully reached into the cabinet and instead of retrieving two white dainty coffee mugs for her and Maggie, she grabbed three. The anticipation built as I watched her pour coffee into her mug and Maggie's before placing them on the table. Then she poured cold Coca-Cola, straight from the

bottle, into my mug, with no ice to break it up, so the dark cold liquid almost resembled coffee. As I joined them at the table, sipping my "coffee" with my pinky raised, I felt so mature. When I sat beside Granny at that kitchen table, it was akin to placing jumper cables on a relational motor—our relationship ignited through shared time in the kitchen, building and growing through each interaction of cooking and eating.

We all have beloved recipes that we remember with adoration—what I like to call heritage dishes. These are the treasured family fare, passed from generation to generation, that never taste quite as delicious as when served by someone you love. For me, it is Granny's toast, homemade French fries, and chocolate cake. It's my mom's homemade spaghetti sauce and my sister's Christmas iced sugar cookies. One bite into these special treats instantly propels us to another time in ways few things can. These memories may transport us to a cherished stage of our lives or call to mind a dear friendship.

When my college roommate, Kimber-Leigh, got married, she and her air force husband dutifully shuffled around the country, first as newlyweds, then as young parents. At each air force base, Kimber-Leigh encountered the daunting task of making new friends, knowing that in two years the moving truck would pull up to the curb and take her away to her next destination. Ever the sentimental and faithful friend, she began to collect recipes as she formed relationships in each new town. Now, twenty years later, as she pulls out her bulging cookbook, she is overcome with memories from deep relationships as well as various locales that she called home.

My childhood friend Shawna also finds recipes to be a connection point. As a young mom and Texas transplant in New York City, birthing a solitary new life in an unknown city often felt isolating. When she discovered a like-minded mom in her apartment building, she quickly set up a weekly playdate. Like any good friend, her neighbor never came empty-handed but always brought her apple crumb cake—and two forks. That breakfast table observed years of tears, laughter, and growth, all shared over plates of crumbly tartness. Years later and back in Texas, Shawna purposely takes out her friend's crumb cake recipe to transport her to that little apartment and the lifelong friendship created over a special dish.

Heritage recipes reach much deeper than our tastebuds. They engage our senses to transport us to special memories. Honoring these recipes can be a powerful method to tell our stories through design. I tapped into this power in my recent home build and designed the butler's pantry using a heritage dish recipe in the decor, creating custom wallpaper based off of my mother's handwritten recipe card. The card has been pulled out, read, spilled on, and handled for more than forty years, with spots from age and tears. I used it just as messy as it appeared, without daring to clean it up. I wanted the wallpaper to show that this recipe card, much like family, was a bit worn and well-loved.

As we observed the build come together in a real-life time lapse, I held my wallpaper idea in secret, waiting to reveal it when the home was finished. When the day arrived, I was elated to guide my family through this personal space in which I designed every detail, a satisfying bookend to that first memory of Grandmother's memorable "I thought you said they were poor" visit to my home. My mom rounded the corner and halted at the butler's pantry, narrowing her eyes at the wallpaper. I watched the realization come over her face as she studied the life-size reproduction of her recipe card that she had cooked with so often.

"Oh!" she exclaimed. "That's my handwriting." She paused and I was curious to see what her first impression of this commemoration of our family would be. She finally spoke. "Wow, I really had good handwriting back then." We laughed and everyone oohed and aahed just as I had hoped.

While wallpapering the pantry may not be possible or desired for some, the truth is that any memento incorporated into the home can carry significance. Some are simple and small and others make a bigger splash—but all are sacred ways to honor your past and tell the story of your family.

These are some of my favorite ways to incorporate family keepsakes in design:

- frame an original recipe card from the family cookbook
- enlarge a photo of the recipe card
- order a custom tea towel, cutting board, or apron with the memorabilia etched on it (Etsy is a great starting point for this. I offer many suggestions on my blog. Find it, along with more resources, via the QR code at the back of the book.)

These tokens do not need to be relegated to kitchen use either. Mementos are some of the best ways to tell your story and can be utilized throughout the home. I will share more in chapter 6.

MAXIMIZING SPACE FOR FLOW AND CONVERSATION

If your kitchen space is lovely but does not function productively, it is about as helpful as printing out the internet. In order to maximize the space, let's discuss where much of the action happens in the kitchen—usually around the kitchen island. No, not the tropical kind, although if we can find a way to bring a part of Hawaii to Texas, I am all for it! If your kitchen configuration doesn't include this space-saver but has the room for one, you might consider adding an island for more prep space. The island is the free-floating area to gather around, sit at, and congregate. Free-floating islands can be purchased online or at the hardware store to fit this need, or if you want to be unique, you can upcycle a beloved piece of furniture or an antique.

No island? No room for one? No worries! Not every kitchen has the open space for an island, or you might just prefer the breathing room that forgoing an island allows. In some cases, not having an island increases traffic flow and ease of access for the work triangle (explained below). Not to mention that omitting an island cuts down on disarray. While we will explore a few benefits of having a kitchen, which I will explain shortly,

they are certainly not the only solution. A long countertop also works well as a landing spot for barstools. It might be that the lack of an island leaves more room elsewhere for an eat-in kitchen.

No matter your island status, here are the most important considerations to maximize the most ideal flow for your kitchen.

Consider the Configuration

The "work triangle," a favored kitchen design concept, consists of the fridge, cooktop, and sink. When planning your kitchen, you want to aim to have these three components in a triangle shape, about four to nine feet apart. This optimum arrangement allows for quick pivots to each station as needed.[1]

Think through Kitchen Traffic Patterns

Before you make changes to your kitchen, think through what areas get congested now and how you might anticipate future traffic jams. For instance, on one previous project, I installed a pull-out trash drawer on the sink side of a kitchen island, and it ended up being the spot where everyone naturally stood for meal prep. Someone would be cutting vegetables and inevitably another family member would need to access the trash and had to ask them to move. Designers make mistakes too. (Designers—they're just like us!) In the next house I worked on, I first determined the natural preparation space and then designed the layout so the trash drawer was on the opposite side.

Add Chairs, Barstools, and Small Seating Options

One side of the countertop can be used for bar-top seating. If you have small children, furniture with stain-resistant fabrics or leather is a helpful feature, especially if the kids spend a lot of time in the kitchen. Remember, don't fret if the paint gets scuffed by little swinging feet at the bar. Paint is simple to touch up, and normal wear and tear happens with kids. Allow your home to serve you, not the other way around.

If your kitchen space is lovely but does not function productively, it is about as helpful as printing out the internet.

Corral the Clutter

By nature, countertops quickly accumulate clutter. To combat this, I reduce the opportunity for piles of things by not housing many items in that space. I then use a basket or tray to corral paperwork. This becomes an easy system for storing mail, homework, and the random assortment of messy infringers so the countertop stays relatively clear.

Action tip: Want to declutter your kitchen in ten seconds? The room will instantly look cleaner if you remove magnets, photos, and flyers from the refrigerator.

Curtail Countertop Chaos

In your personal mess hall, traffic usually breeds chaos. I can offer you a one-way ticket on the Clean Kitchen Train. When it comes to storing items on your countertops, limit what you allow to sit out. If you utilize an appliance less frequently than once a day, store it out of sight. After all, do you keep cereal out on the counter? What if you eat it every day? Just like our breakfast is kept in the pantry, small appliances can also be retrieved from behind a cabinet door. I see many beautiful gourmet kitchens, outfitted with top-of-the-line products and design elements, covered by rows of uninviting appliances—blenders, bread makers, juicers—all lined up, side by side, like small, unattractive soldiers. Rarely do these eyesores need to be displayed. Store those babies away and let your countertops breathe. Remember that the kitchen is already a breeding ground for disorder. If you hide away those bulky contraptions until they're needed, you clear up valuable real estate and let your kitchen design take center stage.

Consider Intentional Seating

When there is room, I add a seating area of cozy sitting chairs to the kitchen. Chairs are an unspoken invitation to stay awhile. Whether it is to talk to the cook or relax for a spell, action happens in the kitchen and by including comfortable seating, conversation is encouraged.

I SAT IN ONE SUCH CHAIR that Christmas Eve as my mom and I stared at the blank chocolate cake. Then I heard a sound. As if on cue, my cocker spaniel, Noel, wobbled around the corner, looking guilty with traces of a frosting mustache on her whiskers. We instantly knew what happened. In my imagination, much like the Wet Bandits who cased Kevin McCallister's house in *Home Alone*, my dog paced the kitchen with the same hunger. With the click of the door locking behind us, this rotund canine somehow hoisted her way onto the countertop and licked the entire cake so clean of frosting, we actually wondered if we had forgotten to decorate it in the first place. Clearly, what this house dog lacked in manners, she made up for in form. The brazenness of the plan she made to "clean" the cake was both impressive and unappetizing. (This led to a family gathering to observe the evidence and a debate over whether the three-second rule applied when the frosting "falls" into the dog's mouth. Do you still eat the cake? What would you do?)

Such is the fabric of what kitchen memories are made of. Through the stories of our lives in the kitchen—the ridiculous, the mundane, the hilarious, and the heartbreaking—you engage in the action of life. If you miss out on the experience, you are relegated to what might be the direst family fate of all—hearing the story told secondhand. Creating a kitchen that tells your story is akin to delivering a personal, engraved invitation to your loved ones to take part in the memories that will be retold for years to come. When you set up your kitchen to better aid in the gatherings held there, you have a front-row seat to the memories that will become part of the next generation's stories.

ACTION STEPS

TO CREATE
YOUR KITCHEN
STORY

Things to ponder: What is your family's heritage dish? How can you incorporate a nod to it in your design? Would adding an island improve the flow of your space?

Create a space that aids in connection and tells your story in the following ways:

- display your family's heritage recipe
- consider adding an island
- anticipate kitchen traffic patterns and plan accordingly
- evaluate whether you are employing the work triangle
- add seating around the island or countertops
- reduce the opportunity for clutter by utilizing trays and baskets and clear your refrigerator of magnets
- keep countertops clean and move any small appliances behind a door
- add cozy seating to aid in conversation

This sweet, widowed client had lived in her house for years and was finally ready to tackle a kitchen update, but she wanted to get the most bang for her buck. When we first met, she confessed she felt "out of her element"—unsure of what type of tile, fixtures, and details to choose.

The brown and creme color pairing was dating the space, so the first change was a sophisticated palette update to crisp gray and white. To maximize her budget, we left the blueprint of the room alone. We even used the original cabinets and only refreshed the doors with a coat of paint. This easily saved thousands of dollars yet made the entire room feel new. Quartz countertops, an updated subway tile backsplash, and new appliances and hardware allowed this space to look brand-new.

feature

WHAT IS YOUR DESIGN AESTHETIC?

MODERN

FARMHOUSE

GLAM

TRADITIONAL

Which elements of a kitchen
are you drawn to?

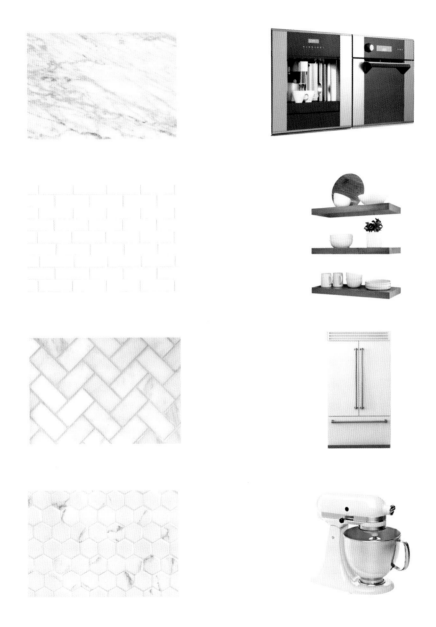

THREE

RECHARGING STORY

The Bedroom

I DON'T HUMILIATE MYSELF OFTEN, but when I do, I prefer to be in front of a live TV camera with thousands of people watching.

One early morning, I stumbled into the TV studio with more makeup on than a pageant girl and my large hair curled and teased. (I do live in Texas, where we believe the higher the hair, the closer to God.) I normally love an opportunity to get dressed up, but the combination of the almost offensively early 5:00 a.m. arrival time and the weight of knowing the segment was live and nationally syndicated made this occasion feel more daunting than exciting. *You're a professional*, I thought. *If all these attractive news anchors can get to the studio while the moon is still out and still form complete coherent thoughts, you can too.*

With nerves flip-flopping in my stomach and the brain fog that comes from waking up at the same time as the people who make breakfast donuts, I shuffled behind the producer to the mark in front of the camera. A beautiful redhead with teeth so white they glowed looked up from her notes with a warm smile and introduced herself as Hilary. At the time, I did not have much experience on camera and the jitters felt overwhelming. *You can do this,* I told myself. *Just pretend you're talking directly to Hilary and having a normal conversation. You have nothing to be nervous about. You know this subject and you're an expert.*

The red light behind the camera flashed on, and before I could ask where I was supposed to look and what I should do with my hands, Hilary introduced me in a smooth newsy delivery. I answered a few questions and then she asked, "What do you recommend to make a room look cozy?"

I exhaled. "Oh easy. Blankets. Any room feels warm and inviting if you soften it with throws on a few of the chairs."

Only instead of "blankets," I heard myself say "blankies." *BLANKIES!?!* Yes, like a five-year-old sucking my thumb, I said the word *blankie* on live, national TV. Like calling a sandwich "sammy" or a chicken meal "nuggies."

Pretend that didn't happen and answer the question again. Don't say blankies. Simply say the word BLANKET *like the grown woman you are.*

"Blankies . . . I mean . . ." I stared straight into Hilary's large doe-like eyes. Then I said it again. "Blankies . . . I mean . . . blankies."

In my mind, a record scratched and all eyes in the room bore through me, with one woman looking away only to giggle behind her hand to her neighbor. That's right. Instead of fixing my toddler mistake, I doubled—tripled?—down and did it again. I actually said "blankie" twice. My face burned as I tried to think of how to fix my error. I drew a blank and stared at my host.

AFTER THE GREAT BLANKIE DEBACLE OF 2018, I learned a valuable life lesson that can guide us as we tell the story of our homes. While I struggled in the delivery of my thoughts on that early morning, the sentiment was still correct. Certain elements instantly bring warmth to a room, and by knowing and utilizing those elements, our sterile rooms begin to develop soft edges. Of all the rooms in the home that need soft edges, our bedrooms top the list.

Do you ever get home from work or turn off your bedside lamp and think, *What a peaceful day. That might as well have been a massage*

> Your home can be the sanctuary in which you get away.

because I feel recharged and relaxed. No. I usually end my day attempting to win a blue ribbon in the nonexistent contest of Most Productive, so I stay up until I collapse into bed because I can't pry my eyes open one more second. Just like the theme song to the '80s TV show *Cheers*, I ask myself, "Wouldn't you like to get away?" I would.

Your home, and specifically your bedroom, can be the sanctuary in which you get away. You deserve to retreat to a place where your shoulders relax and you can settle down. A haven just for you, where you walk through the door and instantly feel a sense of peace overtake you. A soft landing from the hard chaos of the world. That should be your home, and more than that, your bedroom. This space should reflect your favorite things.

However, when I enter potential clients' homes, I frequently notice the primary bedroom is often the last room that gets attention. It's quite common that no matter what season or stage in life, very few adults have finished their bedrooms. If they are parents, you can be sure the kid's room is fully outfitted with all the latest primary color puzzles and ruler growth charts. Yet in total opposition to the oxygen mask rule, the parents don't seem to realize that their room is just as important to complete, if not more. For some, there always seems to be another pressing issue, another event to save money for, a future cost to prepare for. Decorating their bedroom seems frivolous at best, selfish at worst.

It's true that it sometimes feels like life keeps lobbing us financial curveballs. But as Tom Hanks taught us in *A League of Their Own*, there is no crying in baseball. Even when life events throw us off our game, we can meet our families' needs and still make a commitment to invest in ourselves. Consider how home would feel if you had a sanctuary that recharged you. Would that allow you to better provide for others? If the feeling of peace was present when your eyes popped open each morning, wouldn't it help set the tone of your day with less frazzle and hurry? What if you had your own sacred place to read, write, or dream? Perhaps a retreat to regroup and recharge where the noise of the world is a little bit quieter? In my opinion, even if you have to take small steps, carving out a sanctum in your home is the best investment you can make. You are a grown-up. If it is not time for a grown-up room now, when will it be?

WHAT IS YOUR SPACE TELLING YOU NOW?

English was my favorite class growing up. I certainly paid attention on the day we discussed the importance of the setting of the story in a literary work. The setting sets the mood of the book, reflects the current society, influences the dialogue, and can even become a part of the story. Now, imagine that you are the star of the next great feature film and the story commences in your bedroom. How does this story unfold? What does the setting say about you, the main character? Think back to the movie *13 Going on 30*. If you are unfamiliar, the character played by Jennifer Garner,

Jenna, falls asleep in her basement and wakes up in a polished Manhattan penthouse with a closet full of couture clothes. This dreamy apartment was smooth and sophisticated, and that gave a strong testimony to the type of person who inhabited the space. Jenna was an awkward thirteen-year-old when she went to sleep, so with one look at the setting, the audience can instantly deduce that the person who lives there is drastically different. No explanation or dialogue was necessary. The setting said it all.

Now, in the story of you, when the camera pans over your room to capture your first stretch as you climb out of bed, what can we surmise about who you are? Is it a finished room with style authentic to the person it belongs to? Does it set the tone for what you value and how you tackle your day? When the audience sees your room, what will they deduce about you, the main character? Is the space disheveled, incomplete, or dark and drab? If a character woke up in that room, how do you think they would feel? Energetic and ready to tackle the day? Or maybe lethargic and unmotivated?

I believe the spaces we inhabit greatly influence how we feel about ourselves. Perhaps you are an anomaly who has conquered the aspiration for superhuman inner joy from within. If so, you are probably also the lady behind me in the coffee line at 7:00 a.m. who is overly cheerful—and talking a little too loud. But I think most of us are riding shotgun in the emotional roller coaster of life, gripping the seat bar, and some days we feel one step above shelter dog. We typically feel a bit better about starting our day with small wins, like when the dirty dishes are out of the sink or the laundry has been unexpectedly folded and put away already. No matter the grit of our inner reserves, our surroundings influence how we feel. Thankfully, completing our bedrooms to tell our stories is not as difficult as we might believe.

There are several simple and practical ways to tell your story in your room. Here are a few of my favorites.

Incorporate a Cherished Photo or Piece of Art

In the spirit of having a room that appeals to your adult sensibilities, incorporate a cherished piece of art or beloved photo into your decor.

This could be a sentimental family piece or a new item that makes your heart leap when you pass by it. For me, this is a canvas of handmade art that reads: "Be the real deal." The bright colors the artist employed to letter this authentic statement suggest who I strive to be, so much so that when I return to my room and see the canvas, I am gently reminded of the beauty of authenticity. There is something reassuring about resting my eyes on something that delights me each day. Truly, when I walk by it, for that split second, the colorful art and positive sentiment put a little pep in my step and center me.

Is there a quote, verse, or phrase that encourages you? This might be set in a beautiful photo or framed treasure. One of my clients took off on a European pilgrimage and had a spiritual epiphany in a patch of wildflowers. To tell her story, I knew the most crucial piece in the room would be art reminiscent of that flower field. Another client remembers the songs his father strummed out on his guitar on Sunday afternoons. Now, instead of collecting dust in a box, the guitar invokes nostalgia from its perch above the mantel, centered in my client's room. What could this special piece be for you? What piece could you add to your room to tell a part of your story?

Put a Chair in There

Just as in the kitchen, I'm a huge proponent of adding a sitting area to any empty space in your bedroom. It feeds my soul to have a dedicated spot to curl up and read, journal my thoughts, or even sit down and put on my shoes. Since we are all friends, I will also confide that a sitting area can sometimes double as a landing spot to store my clean clothes until they get put away. I initially did not mean for this to be the case, but I relate to a meme that says, "Clothes that are too dirty for the closet but too clean for the laundry: Welcome to the chair." I do have that chair, but mine is actually a couch. It allows me to sit in my bedroom comfortably as I tackle mundane tasks or get a little work done. I like to prop up my feet when I work, so a comfortable seat is an important step for me when I am creating the haven of my space.

Whatever the purpose you determine, having a sitting area in the bedroom is a thoughtful touch that transports the bedroom from a place where you simply sleep to a place where you can also find rest.

Use Textures, Scents, and Soft Throws to Infuse Serenity

Have you ever gotten a gift that seems so extravagant that you refused to use it, because after you did, it would be gone? I hoard bath bombs, candles, bottles of bubble bath, and anything else that makes me feel like a fancy lady. You would think I'm waiting for a glamorous, last-minute invitation to the Academy Awards. They say the first step is admitting you have a problem, so here goes nothing: "I am Courtney and I have a beauty product hoarding issue." The only way I can overcome it is to indulge in lavish self-care. Which is simple for me to tell you to do, after all, since if we do not care for ourselves well, we have no margin to care for others. But the thought of actually having to put those words into action and use my fancy bath bomb gift makes me sweat glitter.

Is there a certain product or activity that makes you feel special? Maybe it is not a bath product but the world's softest robe that you longingly drag your fingers along every time you go to the store. You know the one that is so luxurious that they likely spun it from unicorn giggles. Would it be too crazy to actually buy it? I want to challenge you to find some small way to treat yourself this week, and I will also take the challenge. One of our most important jobs is to care for ourselves, and this is not a job that can be outsourced. As much as our coworkers might appreciate the gesture, we cannot send them to have a massage for us. So, let's decide to be lavish in our self-care to ultimately better serve those we love. This might be as simple as diffusing your favorite scent in your room or lighting the candle that you normally reserve for when guests come over. You are worth it. A smidgen of lavishness might make you feel like Beyoncé. Fortunately, it is easy for us to hold each other accountable. If I see you and you don't smell awesome, I am sending you back through the twelve steps.

The spaces we inhabit greatly influence how we feel about ourselves.

End the Storage Wars

If you share a room with a roommate or significant other, I'd venture to guess that you lean to one extreme or another when it comes to the contents on your bedside table. Either your nightstand is completely empty (so clean that only the occasional tumbleweed floats by) or it is packed so tight with stuff that adding one more thing would make the house of cards collapse. Because God has a funny sense of humor, your partner might have the exact opposite bedside table philosophy. While you may not see eye to eye on clearing away clutter, don't throw in the towel just yet. Save the relationship by investing in bedside tables with ample storage. Having options allows the messy person a place to hide all the cords, tissues, books, vitamins, candles, lotions, lip balms, glasses, etc. in the drawers. (If you wonder to which side my pendulum swings, the list I just made contains everything currently sitting on my bedside table. Guilty as charged.)

Choose Sconces, Not Scones

Are you like me and in desperate need of even more space on the nightstand? Opt for wall sconces instead of lamps. These lights mount to the wall, which allows the bedside table to sit ready for all your junk—I mean, stuff. (I must inject this side note that these are not the same things as scones. Scones are the little biscuits they eat with tea in Britain. I often hear these two terms confused and then have to stifle a giggle while imagining someone reading in bed next to a wall-mounted blueberry baked good.) Using a sconce utilizes dead wall space for lighting and clears up the entire tabletop for your stack of eight books, all of which are important and currently being read at the same time, depending on the mood. If you do not have hardwired outlets already installed by the bed, you can get sconces with plugs, but this means an unsightly wire will be running down your wall to the outlet. If there is no natural way to cover it, I suggest hiring an electrician to hardwire the sconces and avoid visible cords.

Settle the Giant TV Debate for Good

Home thermostats have been set with less negotiation than talks about including a TV in the bedroom. The Anti-Telly camp prefer their bedroom to be technology free, saying it's peaceful (with some even saying it is more romantic). The opposition, Pro-Remote camp, embrace their TV as a preferred method to relax and have a few giggles before bedtime. Those on the far Pro-Remote spectrum have been cited to even sleep with the TV on. Wherever your TV politics fall, embrace this truth and settle the war for good—there is no correct answer. The right answer is the one you feel strongly about. I have designed bedrooms without technology, and I've designed bedrooms with large TVs. I have personally lived in bedrooms both with and without. Some issues are not design-related but are actually just personal preferences. Of course, design can play a part, but the more important factor is considering the practicality of how you live in your home. You get to choose what works best for you and how you relax. If you enjoy having a TV in your bedroom, go for it. If you want to pass, that is great too. In both instances, you can have a lovely room.

THE ELEPHANT IN THE ROOM IS SHAPED LIKE A THROW PILLOW

After working with numerous couples, it has come to my attention that there is a bit of a divide between spouses. That's right, I'm talking about throw pillows. In some households, it's a dirty word.

These decorative pillows just do not make sense to some of you. They have no purpose.

The conversation usually sounds something like this.

"What is the point of them?"

"Looks."

"Do you sleep on them?"

"No."

"So, you just take the little pillows off the bed only to put them back on later?"

"Exactly."

If you are the practical one who does not understand why these tiny pillows exist, I will attempt to summarize this phenomenon here in a gross generalization, using a slow tone to avoid confusion.

Throw pillows are to the primary bed like trim is to the doorway. It is not as useful as it decorative, but if missing, it's akin to an itch one cannot scratch. The nagging sensation will not go away until satisfied. The room is not finished.

Yes, that's correct. You will have to remove these groups of tiny pillows from your bed only to put them back in place later. You are right—it does not make much sense. We all know this. We did not make the rules, we just know them and enforce them. If you listen closely, you may hear evidence of a common rallying cry—

What do we want? Throw pillows!

When do we want them? Now!

Where do we want them? All over the bed!

I can't say that I can explain it any more than that. Some design choices may be better left as a mystery.

UNFORTUNATELY, I had a much bigger issue than deciding whether to adorn my bed with throw pillows while I stared blankly at Hilary in that TV studio. The double-down blankie incident hovered in the air above my head like a cartoon thought bubble. While she probably wanted to prompt me to "use my words," Hilary, always the professional, covered my mistake and somehow even made me look clever.

The lesson I learned during the great blankie debacle is this: We all make mistakes but oftentimes, we are unaware of the good that may arise from them. Hilary's professionalism and cheerful demeanor impressed me so much that I reached out to her after the show. Over the first of many heart-to-heart discussions, we realized one of us had experience in an area the other was facing. She is now a dear friend and I finally know that the reason her teeth are so white is because she doesn't drink coffee.

I also cemented what I am good at and what I am not. This is a valuable lesson and translates to design as well. It's the difference between choosing a victim mindset or embracing a learning posture. For example, most people agonize over choosing a paint color. But a learning posture says if you paint a room an undesirable color (and who hasn't), it's just paint. It is actually very simple to change and comparatively inexpensive to repaint a room. Sure, it might be a hassle, but ultimately, design mistakes are okay. They happen to the best of us, and they will happen to you. They have happened to me. Once I know what areas I am strong in, I can outsource my weak areas to people who are far more qualified to accomplish a task. This leaves me time to fill the roles only I can fill—mom, family member, friend, and business owner.

Because I learned from my experience that day on live TV, I now think twice before I agree to a live interview with such an early shooting schedule. Public humiliation quickly taught me that both my brain and my mouth have a 7:00 a.m. call time requirement.

ACTION STEPS

TO CREATE YOUR BEDROOM STORY

If there was ever a time you deserved a place to recharge, it is now. Follow the action steps from the chapter to create a bedroom retreat that better tells your story.

- Incorporate a piece of art, a photo, or a family keepsake just because it makes you happy.
- Add a space to relax other than your bed—this could be a chair or a couch.
- Incorporate your five senses to create a serene environment.
- Allow yourself to indulge in self-care and start by creating a room where you feel at peace.
- Consider adding sconces if you need more room on a crowded nightstand.
- Never say "blankie" on live TV.

This energetic mom of two had a busy schedule between family responsibilities and a demanding job in the medical field. Like many adults, her bedroom always seemed to fall to the end of the priority list. She had a vision for a personal retreat that felt luxe, feminine, and inviting. To achieve this, we started the stylish refresh by bathing the walls with a soft pink paint, leaving the ceiling white to highlight the arched ceiling. A soft, velvet bedspread housed assorted throw pillows of blush, black, and white to provide color and texture. Rose gold accent tables with carved mirrors flanked each side of the bed and added storage and style. A new chandelier provided extra light, and a tailored bench at the foot of the bed assisted in turning this space into a relaxing, chic getaway.

feature

THREE THINGS THAT ARE DATING YOUR HOME

Time to Take a Fresh Look

Before a guest steps through the threshold at my friend Andie's house, she already knows what they're likely to say. Although she is intuitive, this isn't because she's clairvoyant. She has simply created a catnip-like conversation piece that visitors can't resist commenting on.

A few years ago, when Andie inherited a small, quirky family cabin, the lack of updates was glaring. Linoleum floors, shag carpet, metallic wallpaper—walking through it was like turning to a chapter straight from a 1970s history book. Then she saw the mother of all time capsules, the pièce de résistance—an oversize avocado-green kitchen range. With sleek stainless silver ranges filling current store shelves, she knew this hulking olive-hued piece was a relic.

When updating the space, Andie told me she could not deny the charm of the retro range. It spoke to her as a family artifact, calling to her from another time in history. So now, amid a perfectly executed kitchen renovation, an avocado range proudly stands guard as the best conversation starter in the house. Andie knew the correct way to employ a vintage item, and she included it with intention.

Many of us are unaware of the design decisions dating our homes. Unlike Andie, these old items are not there on purpose. Some of us are living with design decisions we made so long ago that we can no longer see them with fresh eyes.

Action tip: Pretend you are having a party—or actually have a party—and view your space as your visitors would. This will help you see what you have previously overlooked. Because even those with good taste can take a wrong turn.

Even at the risk of stepping on a few design toes, I want to reveal to you what your unobjective eyes could be glossing over. That way, you are not designing from ignorance but are making deliberate choices for your home.

Allow me to suggest a few overused design crutches that could be setting your space back a decade.

TOO. MANY. SIGNS.

As I walked into the kitchen I attempted to follow directions. First they instructed me to *gather*, but I needed to multitask, because I was also supposed to be *living, laughing*, and—of course—*loving*. While I juggled these tasks, I was also encouraged to have *a little bit of coffee and a whole lot of Jesus*. Meanwhile, I needed to remember that *life isn't measured by the amount of breaths we take.*

Did you think it was? Oh no. One look at these walls told me *it is measured by the moments that take our breath away.*

Listen, I love a sign as much as the next person, but sometimes I enter a home and am shouted at by cheesy clichés from every angle. Well-meaning thoughts can turn into overused declarations written in Comic Sans. There is nothing inherently wrong with hanging a sign in your space, but if you live in a farmhouse, you may not need your walls to make that announcement. I am pretty sure the cow pasture and chicken coop gave it away. On the other hand, if you live on a cul-de-sac but love farmhouse *style*, I would contend it would be more effective to *show* it instead of *telling* it. Signs have become a design crutch because they are irresistible, often clever, and oh so true.

Consider our thought process as we get dressed in the morning. Do we wear an iconic T-shirt every day? Hopefully not. Instead, we might throw one on every so often while balancing our wardrobe with classy, neutral pieces and pops of color.

The sign is the equivalent of the iconic T-shirt, and if some homes were an outfit, every piece they wore would shout a different sentiment.

Guide to Follow If a Sign Fits Your Needs

If you are hanging a sign because you love it and it makes your heart beat faster, that is a win.

If you are hanging a sign because it's funny or you are unsure how to fill a space, perhaps you should go back to the drawing board and examine how you could a more original alternative.

Bottom line: limit the signs.

Do not use more than one in a room, and if you can use fewer than that, even better. The idea to embrace is to leave a little space for some mystery and show, don't tell. Use decor that speaks to you. Err toward subtly suggesting your style through example instead of declaring it with a megaphone.

Pair that ideology with an editing session. Then, if you find a sign that truly speaks to your soul, there is room for it. Recently, I displayed a vintage grocery sign in my kitchen. It was an antique from an old-school grocery store. I searched for months to find exactly what I wanted, and it fit perfectly in the space above the windows. I adored it. This is the kind of feeling I want you to get from the signs you hang in your home.

Questions to Ask When You Edit

Have I seen this sign in other homes?

Was this popular five years ago?

If my friend saw this, would they be able to drive to a chain and purchase a duplicate? If yes, is there something more original I could hang instead?

CHRISTMAS LIGHTS AFTER DECEMBER

Every year I see grievous offenders that must make Santa cry. This should go without saying, but, please, for the love of Buddy the Elf, take down your Christmas decorations after the holidays are over. If you pass a Christmas tree on your way to mail your Valentines, I would say that the holiday has come and gone and your home needs to catch up. Show some pride of ownership in your neighborhood and do not go through spring (or worse, summer) with forgotten lights hanging from your roof.

In the same way, if there are porch pumpkins displayed when all the other houses have Easter wreaths up, I promise, your neighbors are wondering why you still have them out, but they're probably too polite to mention it.

So, rule of thumb on Christmas, give yourself a good four weeks to get everything put away. But by the end of January, the grace period has long expired. Take the decor down.

For any other holiday, the grace period is about a week. This decor is not nearly as extensive as Christmas and should not take long, so seven days should be sufficient.

FURNITURE WITH NO VARIETY

Finally, we get to the third culprit. Does everything in your bedroom look identical? Like someone pressed the furniture copy-and-paste key? Did you get roped into purchasing the entire furniture set? Let's put away that big-box mentality and, instead, utilize unique pieces. Why, you ask?

First of all, when every piece of furniture in the room is duplicated, it impedes the opportunity to add variety and character through unique pieces. Second, it looks like everything was bought at one time off the showroom floor instead of curated organically over time. And third, it looks old-fashioned because this is the style our parents and grandparents embraced.

What If I Already Have a Matchy-Matchy Set? If you are like Adam Sandler in *The Wedding Singer* and think this information was better to know yesterday, don't sweat it. It is easy to update your room, keep your favorite components, and swap out one or two things with some-

thing fresh. This could be a vintage item, antique, or new item that coordinates seamlessly.

Follow these steps to mix up the space. First, keep the coordinating nightstands. Symmetry looks clean when flanking the bed. Next, swap out the dresser or chest of drawers (didn't you always think it was "Chester drawers"?) for a different one that coordinates but is not in the set. This could be a painted piece or a wood stain that varies in type or color from the original item. Anything that introduces some variety to the space. Finally, once the update is complete, strong-arm generic design and personalize the room with art or photos that are unique to you.

There, I said it. I played my role as your guide. Now it's up to you. If you are an offender, perhaps even a double offender, take heart. This is a safe place. You can take what you want from the design advice offered and decide how it works for your story.

What is a design trend that is universally loved but lets the air out of your helium balloon? Or what idea will you never grow tired of? It's an interesting discussion, isn't it? I would love to hear your take on it. Please share it with me at www.courtneywarren.com/book.

FOUR

RETROFITTING STORY

The Unconventional Space

I DIDN'T ASPIRE TO BE THE BOX GIRL. As a child, I gravitated toward playhouses. These pastimes seem logical now. As an unknowing yet budding designer, the notion of having a place of my own allured me, a respite in which to put my own decorative stamp and shelter away from the rest of the world. When my mom, after a "back in my day we actually used our imagination" speech, brought me a huge appliance box to make into a playhouse, I willingly did so.

I fashioned windows with my safety scissors and made sure to leave the inside flaps open to act as movable shutters. I commandeered her *Better Homes & Gardens* magazines and cut out flowers, clocks, and other decorative things, then carefully adhered them to the box with glue sticks, outlining them with dull-tipped Sharpies. I colored blades of grass around the outside of my box and glued felt curtains on the inside. As the general contractor of this new home project, I could not rest until the new inhabitants deemed it fit. After all, my Annie doll, Kermit with the moving mouth, and I would not read our books in just any cardboard establishment. Finally, we all stepped into the low one-roomed space together and sat hunched over in the opaque brown-hued darkness that cardboard provides. We did it. Home Sweet Box.

What it lacked in square footage, style, and, well, I guess, light, this makeshift cardboard lean-to made up for in privacy. Although, now thinking back, I am not exactly sure how much escape it really provided me, as the box sat in the middle of the Pepto Bismol pink room I shared with no one else. If someone needed me, they could just as easily get my attention in the box as they could have before. I wasn't any farther away. I had just added an extra step. Now, instead of knocking on my door, they walked into my empty room to knock on the top of my box.

Still, it was mine. Once the renovations were truly finished, I curled up and continued to read my way through the Baby-Sitters Club books, only coming out for snacks. Sitting in my box transported me to another world, albeit a dark and cramped one. Then one day my dad came into my room and told me to get out of the box.

What? I thought. *This is my safe space, my playhouse and it has curtains I made. Do you know what this market is like? Where am I going to find a comparable property? Boxes are flying off the market right now. I have a friend who got eight offers over the asking price for her box. It was a box bidding war!* But he would not budge. I protested. "Mom told me to do it," I whined. No movement there either. One last try. "Where am I supposed to 'live, laugh, love' like all the people say?" Nothing. Apparently, he thought it seemed weird to sleep in a box. So, being the resourceful and determined youngest child, I obeyed him. Kind of.

PERHAPS THAT INNOVATIVE USE OF SPACE in those early years triggered something deep in me, because I now rise to the challenge of meeting practical needs by finding alternative uses for unconventional spaces. Thankfully, I'm now a long way from my days of inhabiting a box. Nowadays this creative skill set is utilized for repurposing an empty dining

Houses, like people, have quirks.

room as a home office or turning an oversized closet into a built-in desk cubby. By serving a family's practical needs, I help them tell their story in a better way.

Let's face it. Houses, like people, have quirks. Even if you design your dream house from the ground up, you may find that it does not meet every need you have. It seems to be the personal experience of anyone who has built a custom house that even when they think they thought of everything, they missed something. I always say people could build the perfect *second* dream home. The first try is more of a first pancake. So, in the same vein of making our houses work for us and not the other way around, let's try to think of what spaces are misused and how we can repurpose them.

REPURPOSING UNDERUTILIZED SPACES

A space that is commonly underutilized is the formal dining room. In my region of the country, builders frequently build these rooms immediately off the entry, so it's often the first room visible upon stepping through the front door. However, many families find they prefer dining near the kitchen, and the formal dining room is grossly underused. In fact, many times it becomes the place to store Amazon packages, workout equipment, homeschool supplies, and subsequently, it becomes an eyesore. Other times it holds a dated, perhaps ugly, dining room set that was passed down because no one else in the family wanted it. Added together, this means the first room in the home is also the most unattractive. (Happy first impression: "Welcome to my home! We keep the ugly stuff up front.") Part of my work with clients is to transform unused rooms into spaces with purpose and style. Because this highly visible room is open to other areas, it's crucial to ensure it is attractive, inviting, and clutter-free.

Speaking of areas with unlimited potential, let's also take a look at the spare bedroom. Obviously, if you have guests or family visiting and you think spooning with them on the couch would be awkward, a guest room is a godsend. But what if you live close to all your family and friends and the guest room is gathering dust? Or perhaps you have more than one guest room and the others are sitting empty? Maybe you don't even like anyone in your life enough to have them stay over. (Okay, that was a joke. Sorta.) Well, options abound, dear friend. Even better, with the right design, any ho-hum spare room can be elevated to a purposeful room that is as striking as it is efficient. Allow me to grease the wheels of your imagination and share a few spare room re-creations that tell my clients' stories.

My client Paula had a drab overflow room full of cast-off furniture. It was like the island of misfit upholstery. Rumor was one look at the dated carpet would burn your eyes, so most of the time this room sat empty with the door closed. As an active empty nester and a hustling business owner, she was frankly too busy to give thought or attention to this space, but it irked her that it was underutilized. Her precious husband, admittedly not

Any ho-hum spare room can be elevated to a purposeful room that is as striking as it is efficient.

always the best gift giver—I believe I overheard a mumble about an iron for the last anniversary—saw redemption in his future and gifted Paula a room makeover as an anniversary surprise. Elated, she gave me full rein, pointed me toward her inspiration colors and lighting and storage needs, then made me keep the rest a secret until it was complete.

With her love for bold colors in mind, I began the transformation by updating the boring beige paint to a deep peacock teal. Paula had a growing collection of her favorite designer purses sitting forgotten in a dark closet. Recognizing this collection was part of her story, I brought them out into the light and grouped them on one wall to act together as a work of art. Repurposed antiques now held her organized supplies, builder-grade lighting was updated to a vintage chandelier, and the worn carpet was replaced with new hardwood-like tile. However, the final missing piece to tie this room together was the detail I giddily planned behind the scenes. It didn't take long to learn of all the hats Paula wore, her favorite was being Mimi to her grandchildren. As I observed the twinkle in her eyes when she spoke of them, I knew the truest way to tell Paula's story was to incorporate her status as Mimi.

After pondering the best way to highlight this beloved role, I commissioned custom art to christen her workspace wall and coordinate with the colors she loved so much. When it was time for the reveal, Paula walked into the room and saw a piece of art that read "Mimi's Mercantile." Her mouth dropped in elation and shock! She looked around the room with glee as she took in the details that made the room shine. Where this dead space was once overlooked, it was now transformed into a stylish home office simply by adding a fresh coat of paint, new lighting, accessories, and simple furniture updates. What was once an afterthought in the house now held a function and told her story.

Another humble bedroom got a makeover so drastic that it's hard to believe the before and after photos show the same space. This active and involved client often hosted her grandkids in a spare bedroom that sorely needed an update. She wanted them to have a cheery landing spot that felt like a home away from home when they came to visit. To initiate the change, I chose navy paint to transform the short ceiling by drawing the eye up and making the room appear bigger. (This is a helpful tip when faced with a low ceiling—paint it!) The small window ledge became a window seat simply by adding upholstered pillows and curtains. Brightly colored

graphic art spelling out "PLAY" hung as a declaration that this updated room was one of fantasy and exploration.

Repurposing space is rarely more useful than when applied to rental space. In many large cities real estate is at a premium. Many people are maxing out their budget to acquire minuscule spaces that are not always the best configuration for their family. Because of this, renters find themselves having to be savvy to utilize all the square footage they can, sometimes in unexpected ways. In one such case, a family of four had two bathrooms in their cramped apartment, and their new arrival meant they now needed a nursery as well. As they began to brainstorm options, they discovered they could easily all share one bathroom and convert their extra bathroom into a nursery for the baby. (This family gets the innovative DIY award, amirite?) Since there was little floor space, they secured a hanging baby bed above the bathtub. While unconventional, it utilized every inch and allowed the baby to sleep peacefully, away from the noise of the city and older siblings.

HOW TO CREATE A SPACE
THAT WORKS FOR YOU

I could tell story after story of repurposing a space to better fit a family's needs. An unused landing becomes a homeschool study space. A home office becomes a bakery headquarters. A media room becomes a music jam room.

Do you sense a pattern? After all, is it logical to purchase furniture we will never use to complete the look of a space we will never eat in? Hopefully you agree that doing so sounds ridiculous. So why do we feel compelled to stage a room we won't use? When we consider our family's needs, we may find a more effective use of space than the default setting of the last owner.

Now it's your turn. What do you *really* need in your home that you don't currently see a way to include? A home office? A space for all your plants? To best evaluate your needs versus your available spaces, simply follow the rules of brainstorming.

1. There are no dumb ideas. Go crazy. Be wild. Treat this exercise like your fifth-grade diary. No one is going to see it. If it makes you feel better, you can start it with "Dear Diary." Think about your deepest desires for your home and who you have a crush on. On second thought, just talk about your home.

2. Pretend like money is no object. Even though it will eventually factor into your decisions, right now we are trying to best decide what you want and need. Limitations will only slow you down. Once you are aware of your needs, then we can brainstorm how to practically make them happen.

Write down all the ideas you can think of on a sheet of paper, answering the following questions.

- Consider your career, family life, or other roles you fill. What change could you make in your home that would make a significant difference or meet a need?
- What one thing could save you time or money, if you had it in your home?
- What skill or hobby could you foster in yourself or your loved ones if you only had the space?
- What change could you make in your home that would wildly increase satisfaction for you or someone you love?
- What would you be willing to risk or fail at to accomplish this in your home?

On another sheet of paper, consider what space sits unused.

- If carpet filled your home and you vacuumed today, which room would still have the vacuum tracks next week? (Evaluate closets, attic or basement spaces, guest rooms, landings, bars, and other such areas. Are you squeezing every bit of function out of those spaces? If your house usage was evaluated with a grade, would you squeeze by, barely passing, or would you be the valedictorian?)
- Why don't you use this space?
- What one thing would make it easier to use this space?

Now compare the two papers. Can anything on one paper meet the needs of the other?

Please note: It is perfectly normal if nothing comes to mind right away. The most magnificent idea usually pops into my head at the most mundane times—while my mind is at rest, I'm in the shower, or I'm sitting in traffic. Allow yourself to ponder these questions for about a week, revisiting the papers every few days. Does anything rise to the surface?

CLEAR AND DEFINED SPACES

One of my favorite stories of repurposing a space was for a client whose sixteen-year-old daughter, Kali, was on the fast track to become a professional ballerina. She catapulted forward in her career, training in New York and flying back to Dallas to see family and friends on breaks. When COVID hit, the flights stopped, and Kali faced not being able to return to her crucial classes.

Thankfully, a large empty landing sat outside her bedroom door. With supportive parents and a bit of ingenuity, we realized this large dead zone could easily be transformed into a training area. We laid a brick treatment on the wall to set this hallway area apart from its surroundings, then installed a floor-to-ceiling mirror and barre. Three clocks were aligned horizontally, labeled with the time zones of her friends around the world.

Kali's reaction to the new studio area was great: "It certainly was well used during the COVID shutdown! I rolled a layer of Marley on the floor, set up Zoom classes on the desk in front of the mirror, and did my best to continue to train, despite the chaos of the moment! This space turned into a refuge for me." This innovative use of an unused area helped Kali live her story, and it tells the story of the discipline and training it's taken to achieve her calling.

You will notice that in each of these examples, the purpose of the space is well thought out and does not allow for anything else in the room. Repurposing a room has little margin for error. I am reiterating this point because the biggest risk I see in repurposing spaces is the potential that it turns into a disaster zone. It feels like the parenting equivalent of allowing your teenager to have one friend over when you leave town and fearing you might come home to a wild house party. In a similar "giving you an inch" scenario, the encouragement to redefine a room's purpose is not a veiled suggestion to allow for indoor chaos. In fact, while restyling a room to serve a new purpose, it should be even more clear and defined. If not done well, it might look like Cousin Eddie from *Christmas Vacation* left the RV in the driveway and set up shop in your dining room.

What do I mean? Let me give you a practical example. In one scenario, I might recommend a treadmill in the dining room, but in another, it would be an enormous faux pas. For instance, it does not work for the Peloton to be nestled between the dining table and the china cabinet. However, if the treadmill is in the "dining room" because it is surrounded with other gym equipment, that appears intentional. It's worth the extra time and attention it takes to ensure a space looks cohesive when you repurpose it.

I only feel confident in advising you to break design rules if it's done in a well-thought-out and intentional way. If you lack the time or follow-through to finish the repurposed room, it is better to leave the room in its original form. Like your dad preaches, do it right or do not do it at all.

SPEAKING OF DADS, after mine informed me I couldn't hang out in my box away from home anymore, I quickly set my sights on a new locale. One with a door. There was an unused storage closet under the stairs, so I asked for permission (from my mom; I am no fool), and soon my new and improved "playhouse" began to take shape.

Since this room was nestled directly under the stairs, it had an awkward sloping ceiling overhead. Limited outside light created a vast midnight mood even deeper than the darkness of the box. But the first construction project I oversaw had only sharpened my design skills, so I upgraded this space by sticking lime-green glow-in-the-dark stars to the stair-shaped ceiling with gummy tacks. The stars would have glowed, too, if they ever saw the light of day. But I could manually light them up with a flashlight, a task that required holding the bulb to each individual star at a ninety-degree angle above my head. Despite the burning in my forearms, I was satisfied by the light of the artificial sky. I lugged extra pillows and blankets into the room, and while I had to sit at an unnatural angle, craning my neck to read with the same flashlight, the location seemed more exclusive than my box. After all, isn't that what experts say to look for in real estate?

Did I seem eccentric? Maybe a little. I do consider myself pretty quirky. But looking back, I can now see what my father overlooked. With a little more foresight, I think he would have discovered that what he considered an irregularity was actually a skill in the making. On a very small scale, I had the ability to see a space with little benefit, cast a vision for what it could be, then turn it into something useful. Twenty years later, that is what I do every day. What was interpreted as a childhood quirk was actually a premonition of my future calling.Keep that in mind as we tell the story in our next space.

Just because a homebuilder or previous owner used a room for one function does not mean we have to use that space the same way.

ACTION STEPS

TO CREATE YOUR UNCONVENTIONAL SPACE STORY

Complete the chapter's activity by answering the questions on page 105 on two pieces of paper.

Consider what unused area may be better utilized in your home. What would it take to upgrade this area into what you need it to be?

Time for a check-in. We are halfway through the journey of understanding how to tell the story of your home.

- What takeaway jumps out at you?
- Of the first chapters of the book, which resonates most with you?
- If you started tomorrow, which project would you take on?

before

This pale pink spare bedroom was underutilized and overlooked. My client wanted to turn it into a playroom for her grandchildren, but execution felt elusive. As a home decor shop owner, she rarely had trouble decorating her spaces, but because her grandchildren had varied interests, creating a cohesive design was causing a dilemma. Replacing the boring beige carpet with clean white herringbone tiles instantly made the room feel bigger. I knew using a bold color palette would reinforce the youthful energy of the room. A red ceiling, turquoise detailing, and pops of black, white, and pink admittedly sounded a little crazy when I suggested it, but my client

trusted the vision and ended up loving it. The grandchildren's handy firefighter dad made the beds—a special resting place for each of them, flanked on opposite ends of the room. Keeping my client's fondness for vintage artifacts in mind, I included special mementos for her grandson, like a firetruck ladder, wheels, a sign from an old firehouse, and some of his dad's personal items. We even found an authentic, vintage fire extinguisher. Not to be outdone, the princess bed was surrounded by fairy lights and colorful pom-poms that hung from the ceiling. This room also included a reading nook with a hanging swing and an art table for their next creative endeavors.

HOW TO MAKE A RENTAL FEEL LIKE HOME

A Rental Can Still Tell Your Story

Sometimes buying a permanent home is not in your best interest. Renting gives you freedom in future options. But do you feel that the minute a lease is signed, you have also been sentenced to design jail? Thankfully, rentals are no longer where design goes to die. There are many temporary ideas you can use to make the space feel like home. Follow these simple steps to feel right at home at your new address.

FOCUS ON WHAT YOU CAN CHANGE

Rules are rules, right? It probably hurt when you had to sign the contract and agree not to use paint on the walls. How dare they?! Yet, with a glass-half-full mindset, let's focus instead on what you *can* do to make the space your own.

Instead of bringing in color with wall paint, how about you paint a striking piece of furniture in a bold hue? Or add dramatic curtains for the pop of color you are looking for? Color is not just subject to your walls, and there are many temporary ways to personalize a space.

Does your bath look more like the decade of the moon landing than the decade of SpaceX? Perhaps you have old vintage bathroom tile, complete with a pink sink or green tub. Embrace it! Pair it with a contrasting accent color and make the most of that funky tile. Provide the accent color through the shower curtain, hand towels, bath mat, and wall art, making sure to incorporate a bit of the tile color with it. Suddenly the vintage tile looks intentional and is a definite conversation piece.

The name of the game is to find a creative way to make the most of what you have. There are still many options besides wall paint and new tile, and this is a great time to find that untapped creativity and bring it to life.

EMBRACE THE TEMPORARY

Gone are the days of permanent choices in design. Peel-and-stick tile, wall decals, and temporary wallpaper will give you the look you desire without large-scale renovation. When you move, simply peel your decor off the wall and it will be like it never happened.

When you wish you could change your flooring, do it—by using rugs. Rugs can break up an open floor plan into separate areas, or they can be layered to provide texture and interest on top of otherwise dismal flooring. Toss one under a coffee table, dining table, or reading nook—or all three. Rugs are a relatively inexpensive way to add a drastically different color and pattern to the area.

OPEN UP OPTIONS WITH OPEN SHELVING

Hang floating shelves as the base and use them to house various items throughout the year. Floating shelves leave minimal holes in the wall and leaning decor on them will provide so many design options without any permanent decisions. Suddenly you'll be able to change out your decor each season with minimal work or wall patches.

KEEP LOOKING UP

Instead of simply repeating what worked in your last space, utilize high ceilings (if you have them) and bring your storage up. Install a tall bookshelf, a cabinet above the toilet, or a loft bed with storage space underneath. Resist the temptation that everything must be on the floor to be accessed and leave more room for activities.

Signing a lease does not mean you have to say goodbye to your personal style. Use your cool new locale to embrace design ideas that would have never been possible in a more traditional space. Even better, use this time to do something bold you have always wanted to do. You will likely not live here forever, so have fun with it. After all, if design is not fun, we are doing it wrong.

FIVE

PLAYING STORY
The Kid Rooms

ONE THING I ENJOY about helping people with design is that the variety of my clients is as vast as the hues on a paint swatch. They come from all ages, life stages, and demographics. A majority of them have a child, whether it's one who lives at home, one who visits frequently, or one who fills another special role like godchild, niece, nephew, foster kid, mentee, grandkid, and the like.

If you have no need for knowledge on how to best create a children's room, this is a great time to go get a snack and meet me in the next chapter. Remember, you won't use all the tips at the same time, so this content will sit safe and warm if you ever need it down the road.

I didn't realize that the minute I became a parent, I must have signed a contract to agree to unsolicited advice. Random strangers have actually told me the reasons why they did not like our baby's name. I have been regaled with all kinds of philosophies on how to soothe an infant or discipline a toddler. Never one to follow the crowd, I decided to subscribe to my own parenting philosophy based on cuteness. I called it "get my way while I can." This consisted of taking advantage of my kids' youngest years by choosing the most adorable baby options—for outfits, party themes, and room decor—before they had strong opinions and wanted their own way.

For instance, remember when mustaches were all the rage a few years ago? I was already busy pinning photos on invitations with puns like "I mustache you a question" when my son told me he wanted a detective birthday party. "Sounds great," I said. Surely every great crime solver's first line of defense is a woolly mustache. This additional detail was only so I could decorate the party with the current creative decor and satisfy my internal party planner. Once he got older, I knew I would be quelling my inward desire to plan something creative, like a sock monkey party, for the latest Marvel character, so I encouraged my ideas before he was too old to think his were better.

Because the thing they do not tell you about kids is, they grow. Soon those sweet baby coos turn into opinions. Really bossy opinions. And if you aren't careful, you'll have a mild case of toddler PTSD from being bossed around by a tiny irrational dictator who is hysterically sobbing at his third birthday party because you asked him to say thank you with real words instead of barking like a dog. At this point, it's not so easy to create a room that everyone can agree on. So, when your child is old enough to care, how do you decorate their room in a manner that lets you both get your way?

HAVE YOU EVER FELT the underwhelm of visiting a childhood location as an adult? I recently returned to my elementary school after many years. When I was a colt-size, permy-headed brace-face, the cafeteria loomed larger than a football field. Decades later, as a four-eyed grown-up, I thought it looked dinky and quite similar to any other room that served square pizza on Fridays. When I removed my child goggles, the room shrunk in size and the wonder dissipated.

Those early lenses were powerful. I like to think of that viewpoint as childhood magic. Can you think back to that time when you believed ghost stories, loved to dress up, or still thought cheesy dad jokes were hysterical? When I was a kid riding in the car as my brother drove, my eyes would bulge out and I would explode with applause when he lifted his hands off the wheel. I did not understand how cars worked and mistakenly

thought taking your hands off the steering wheel for a split second would cause the car to veer off the road and end in a fiery crash. I sat nervously entranced as I watched him dramatically perform this driving magic and was confident he would next reach behind my ear to reveal a fresh lemon stuffed with a dollar bill from my wallet. Such a small thing to be impressed by, but such is childhood. Being a kid is so powerful that, for a very short time, everything seems like it's sprinkled with a little fairy dust.

That wondrous magical delight is why I adore creating children's rooms. The adolescent room is the one ingrained in memory years later. It's the space where nostalgia resides and where rites of passage pave the rocky path to adulthood. If we can create a magical space for a little person, they might just feel how loved they are, how cherished they are, and how wanted they are. A well-loved little person can grow up to be a big person who can take on the world. A childhood room is no small thing.

As I grew, my chosen space grew as well. By middle school, both the box and the dark closet had been traded in for an entire game room. I knew it was something special because it even had a light. Looking back, I realize that by providing these spaces for me, my parents allowed me to unleash my imagination and planted the seeds of a budding designer. Much like J. R. R. Tolkien mused with fellow writers at the old pub in town, my rooms became my creative wellspring. (Yes, friends, I am J. R. R. Tolkien in this scenario. Obvi.)

For instance, one of my long-standing dreams was (and still is!) to design a clothing line. My room became my design studio. Every inch was covered with creativity. I turned extended window soffits into a canvas inspiration board for my new creations, all cut from magazines. I assembled collages, packed tight to fill the entire space, with overlapping cutouts of unique color combinations, inspiring ensembles, and rad '90s styles, then covered every wall with them from top to bottom.

I like to think I was an early promoter of upcycling. I think we all were back then. Just like we have now deemed "cheese plates" the more cutting-edge name of "charcuterie board," upcycling used to simply be called "using hand-me-downs."

My friends and I didn't share cigarettes. That was not our vibe. We shared puff paint. So, when my mom upcycled her navy velvet armchairs, we passed around the bucket of puff paint bottles, each carefully choosing a color to document the moment. We lettered our monikers along the straight legs and under the rectangle arms of the chairs, graffiti names scrawled in neon pinks and greens. Only after it dried did we learn that puff paint is actually a misnomer, as it is more stiff and scratchy, which resulted in the chairs

becoming more of a statement art piece than practical items. After sitting in the newly designed chairs, our legs were peppered with light pink scratches like we lost a fight with a street cat. But the chairs were unique and creative, and, well, when you are thirteen, chairs that look cool hold more value than chairs that accomplish the one reason they have for existing.

One summer, I painted a mural on a half wall in my room, with my favorite quote surrounded by bold primary colors. I cannot imagine letting my middle school child loose with open paint cans, wet paint, and paintbrushes on carpet—but parenting rules were different in the olden days. People smoked on planes and in hospital waiting rooms, and parents let kids walk to the store alone to buy candy cigarettes. Mostly, there was just a lot more smoking back then and perhaps fewer seat belts. So, I guess painting a Bible verse on the wall was hardly worrisome. As a result, this room became a playground for me and instigated embers of creativity that I still call on today.

CREATE KID'S ROOM MAGIC

What does it mean to allow a child's room to be magical? How do adults go about supporting this? Does creating a magical room mean that they take the reins or that we succumb to every whim and trend and redecorate every time their obsessions change?

To solve the quandary of how much input children deserve in their room, I would like to call your attention to a notepad sitting next to me in my home. When visitors, family, and friends come over, they can sign this notepad, jot down what they're thankful for, and use it as a guest book. In all different handwriting, with various shades of color, thoughtful answers

are penned over several months of guests in my home. It is much like a grown-up version of my navy chairs, without the puff paint.

Some of the items read *I am thankful for . . .*

family

friends

feeling good

health

faith

But one of the words looks different from the rest. With John Hancock swag and much larger, messier letters, a childish scrawl leans to one side and reads "POOP." There is a little boy in my family who is thankful for poop. Apparently, we give a young boy a writing utensil and all bets are off. So, the short answer is no. We cannot hand complete design control over to these poop-grateful tiny terrorists. But we can include them in the story of their rooms.

CREATE A ROOM THAT WILL GROW WITH THEM

We want to take their input, loves, passions, and interests and translate them into a room that is exciting without letting them call all the shots. The following are a few ways I ensure the look of my kids' rooms stays timeless.

Keep Big-Ticket Furniture Purchases Neutral

The name of the game is to use large furniture as long as possible. After all, these are the priciest items, so we want to keep them neutral, without themes or crazy colors. In the same way that everything goes with a pair of jeans, beds and dressers will follow suit if kept to a color and style that can transition as the room matures.

Remember, nursery furniture is not used for long, so opt for cribs that convert to big-kid beds. For a changing table, consider fastening a changing pad to a student desk. The drawers can hold diapers and supplies. Later, your child will have a desk when they need it. Also, a neutral upholstered nursery rocker could find a new home in your den after baby-cuddling days are over.

Compromise on a General Theme, Then Add Smaller Specifics

My son wanted to paint his room the inviting colors of blue and black to root for our home team, the Dallas Cowboys. While I like these hues individually, I envisioned my ten-year-old residing in a life-size bruise. And I had questions. Would he still want a Cowboy room during the NBA season? Plus, that blue and black paint would not transition to another design without repainting. I faced a dilemma as a mom who is also a designer. How did I give him what he wanted without it looking hideous?

To compromise his need for cool and my need for style, I took a component of his idea—football—and together we created a vintage sports room. I scoured markets and eBay to find vintage pennants, photos, and jerseys and placed them with coordinated pillows and quilts to reinforce the theme. We kept the room clean and white and allowed the vintage pennants to introduce color, then planned the bedding around those hues. Once we determined the main areas of the room, we added some specific posters to root for the Cowboys, and guess what? He loved it, and I loved that he had a stylish room that would not be obsolete in six months.

So, go easy on the themes and bring in just a dose of your child's favorite things with additional accessories, some whimsy, and some color.

Embrace Color Instead of Characters

When a child has an interest, use it strategically. Most of the room should be made up of neutrals or more solid general decor. For example, if your daughter loves the movie *Frozen*, perhaps use colors reminiscent of the movie, such as teal and purple. Next, highlight the specific theme with a simple throw pillow or poster, perhaps an Anna plush and an Olaf beanbag. By keeping most of the decor neutral with inexpensive themed accents, the room can transition nicely to the child's next phase. Then when they move on, you can "let them go" for the next big trend they want to embrace. (Did you see what I did there?)

In my son's case, because we kept the trendy items minimal and inexpensive, it was an easy upgrade to a room that fit his next obsession. The vintage sports memorabilia–inspired decor easily transitioned to his preteen years, then to his teenage years.

When a child has an interest, use it strategically.

Consider an Accent Wall or Wallpaper

Paint is the least expensive solution that also makes the biggest impact. Talk about a win-win. It's like ordering tater tots and getting a few fries in the bag. Use paint to create an accent wall or special design. Stripes, chevrons, rainbows—by using paint, a simple wall can turn into a wow-factor focal point. I used this philosophy when a national vacation rental company contacted me to design several rental units. I had free design rein (yay!) but had to stick to a tight budget to adhere to their investment goals. My goal was to make their rentals an exciting space that out-of-towners would flock to, so I had to discern ways to get the biggest bang for their buck. When I considered the most inexpensive change that would make the biggest impact, it was paint, hands down. In some cases, I use paint instead of buying furniture. For instance, in a bedroom paying homage to the State Fair of Texas, I added interest to the walls with painted stripes in contrasting bold colors instead of buying a large headboard and art. Doing so elevated a simple bedroom to one with unique personality. By utilizing painted accent walls in each bedroom, I saved the vacation rental business tons of decorating dollars by not purchasing decor. This is a savvy choice in a child's room as well. The invaluable quality of paint is that it can transform the space for the cost of a bucket of paint and a free afternoon. When your fickle darling is ready for something new, it's as simple as picking up a brush.

Incorporate Storage for Your Own Sanity

I'm sure you've noticed kids have stuff. So. Much. Stuff. It seems the younger the child, the bigger the stuff. When I had toddlers, my living room almost seemed to be decorated in primary colors, with accents of plastic and oversized. Balls, cars, blocks, kitchens, rocking horses, dress-up outfits—the list is as long as the carpool line on the first day of school. Stuff overtakes our living room, spilling into the hall and leading a trail all the way back to their room. Giving your kids places to easily stow their

A Note
BEFORE USING WALLPAPER

Using wall decals and wallpaper requires a little legwork before getting started. First, answer important questions like, Who will install it? How much do I need? Does the wallpaper hanger only work with certain kinds of paper?

Wallpaper hanging seems to be a dying profession. In my experience, these people can be picky about what they like to hang and which jobs they'll take. Most professional installers in my area don't like working with murals, decals, or products with sticky backs—so much so that they have refused jobs. I've learned to confirm these details before I purchase any product. After all, if I have cute wallpaper but no one to hang it, it's not going anywhere.

I also do not order wallpaper before having a professional measure the space and verify the quantity of rolls needed. Wallpaper measurements are about as easy to understand as figuring out which remote turns on the TV and which one starts Netflix. In the same way, wallpaper is offered in different mediums.

I once ordered one type of wallpaper only to find that the wall was quoted for the other unit of measurement. The job was put on hold until I could order the correct quantity. When measuring, you also must account for waste and overage. In addition, more wallpaper than you might imagine is used because the seams have to line up and repeat. With all these factors, measurements get tricky. It took only a few wallpaper mix-ups to teach me to leave the details to a paid professional.

stuff will help prevent meltdowns—yours AND theirs—when it comes time to clean up. Whether it's a reconfigured closet or built-in or wall-hung shelves, make sure there's a place for all the important things.

Introduce Magic

Once the theme of the room is established, colors are chosen, and neutral big-ticket items are in place, how does one create childhood magic? It is not exactly something you can "add to cart" for two-day shipping online.

This special aura is not as elusive as you might think. A single dad delighted his daughter by allowing her to sleep under the soft glow of twinkling lights strung above her bed. In a space-themed room, I incorporated a star caster that re-created the Milky Way on the ceiling, projecting small, glowing dots that moved about the room, much like the constellations floating in space. Specialty lights create ambiance and mood, and I have yet to meet a child who does not love them. It is a tried-and-true method to infuse a magical element in a child's room.

However, lights are just one element of magic. Don't be afraid to get creative when it comes to what your child loves. When I asked one mom what her theater-loving daughter would want most in her room if there was no limit, she joked, "A stage." Since the girl's room had a bit of extra space, I began to envision what it would take to include a stage for her to practice her school plays. Though the idea was sparked by a joke, I could make it a reality. I hired a carpenter to build a small platform and hung plush velvet curtains on either side, because what is a performance if heavy curtains do not open dramatically? Now, with her youngest siblings in the audience, my client's daughter wards off stage fright by rehearsing her upcoming roles.

What does your child love? Is there a way to incorporate that interest in their space in a creative way? Perhaps an unexpected element, like a bike, could be mounted on the wall over their bed. In my son's sports room, an authentic vintage scoreboard and lockers from my high school were incorporated to create the feeling of a basketball locker room.

Don't be afraid to get creative when it comes to what your child loves.

TELL THE STORY OF THEIR CHILDHOOD

Many of the stories I think I remember about my past are based on me remembering a photo of them. Have you found that to be true for you? I have long seen this effect in my own life, and it turns out, research confirms it. Elizabeth Loftus, a psychological science professor at the University of California–Irvine says, "Memories fade and can become contaminated without a visual record backing them up. A photo is an excellent vehicle to take you back to a moment."[1]

Because of this, I surround my kids with photos that remind them of exciting times spent with our family, important milestones in their lives, and kind words that people have spoken over them. I also celebrate their lives by incorporating their keepsakes in their space—at least, as long as they will let me without feeling like it's uncool. The story I reinforce through decor becomes "you are treasured and valued," and I want every interaction they have with their space to remind them that they are surrounded by love.

The following are some of my favorite ways to tell a child's story. Because there are many that are appropriate for different stages of childhood, you likely will want to vary them and spread them out over the years. These mementos tell a beautiful story of a child.

Shadow Boxes

Shadow boxes are to memories like chips and queso are to Mexican food. You don't *have* to start with them, but it makes everything that follows better. Using shadow boxes is a lovely way to show off treasured items that are too bulky for a flat frame.

Mementos to frame in a shadowbox might include:

- newborn gowns, baby shoes, and hats, along with a photo
- parents' baby clothes
- parents' childhood Bibles

Photos of family vacations, special events, dear friends, and milestone events take on elevated importance when displayed in a shadow box.

For kids, it is easy to scroll through social media and wonder if other kids have a better life. After all, adults easily fall into the same comparison trap, and we know better (or, at least, we should). I help jog my kids' memories, that they too are living a #blessedlife, by displaying photos of special times, vacations, and people who love them. When that does not work, I yarn long-winded tales of how I walked uphill in the snow to school, wearing headgear and holding a Lisa Frank Trapper Keeper, and they instantly transform into grateful angels who write a thank-you note for every birthday gift.

Family Mementos

Using a favorite item from a relative's childhood is a very sweet throwback and a tangible way to say, "We are connected. You are mine."

My dad's football number, team photo, and state award medal were perfect additions to adorn my son's football room. Including items with a history reinforces heritage and belonging and helps the child understand their family members are real people who share things in common with them.

Framed Birth or Adoption Announcement

This announcement is the equivalent of beaming parents screaming from the mountaintop, "WE DID A GOOD THING AND WE WANT YOU TO KNOW!" The good thing = your kid. Display their announcement, along with a photo, as proof that they really were that little once.

Handwriting Samples for Each Child at the Same Age

If you have a sample of your handwriting from childhood, display it. I have snippets of my boys' writing from second grade, framed next to a sample of their dad's handwriting. If you don't have this, it is not too late to take a sample of their handwriting now. For those younger folk, back in the olden days, handwriting is how we communicated when we weren't texting. I am sure this sounds confusing, so I won't even mention cursive.

Special Items from Birth

When I was expecting both of my boys, I prepared for their arrival by making keepsake gifts. I wasn't the kind of pregnant woman who glowed, or even dimly shone, but I could craft with the best of them. I decoupaged

a keepsake box for one son and painted a plate for the other, and they still sit on their respective bookshelves.

Photos with Family Members

I especially like to frame photos with siblings because I find it never hurts to reinforce sibling love. (Look, kids, one time you liked each other enough to stand side by side and smile. Can you imagine?) Grandparents and other family members are also special relationships to reinforce the message that the children are dearly loved and valued.

Trophies and Other Awards

Kids usually take pride in their hard work, and rightly so. By displaying their awards, we reinforce that we cheer them on in their interests.

Photos of the Parents and the Child at the Same Age

Most kids are fascinated to hear that their eyes favor their dad or they have their mom's smile. Framing side-by-side photos of child and parent provides visual evidence for our kids to learn what we looked like at the same age and how they favor us.

WHAT IS REMARKABLE ABOUT KIDS' SPACES is how much said kids take pride in them. Having a unique room is a surprising banner that children wear, and it's not difficult to tell their story in a way that keeps everyone happy. Because children matter. Their spaces matter. Telling their stories matters. There are so many ways to incorporate their stories in their spaces, and the efforts we make will hopefully reinforce their value to us as they grow.

ACTION STEPS

TO CREATE
THE STORY OF
A KID'S ROOM

As you brainstorm how to tell the story of a child in your home, consider the following questions:

- What kind of room would your child want if they had free rein?
- Is there is a way to incorporate their choice into their room?
- What item could you add to create magic?
- What is one way you could bring their story and their family heritage into their room? Choose one to use now:

  - shadow boxes
  - childhood toys
  - family memento
  - framed adoption or birth announcement
  - handwriting samples
  - newborn memorabilia
  - special photos or awards
  - side-by-side photo comparisons

This client frequently had sleepovers with her grandkids but didn't feel the old-fashioned guest bedroom reflected their fun and playful spirits. The clunky queen bed took up most of the room, and the matching bedroom suite hogged the rest. We swapped the oversized furniture for a sofa with a comfy pull-out couch. The existing taupe hue wasn't doing this dark room any favors, so we traded it in for a bright white that highlighted the natural light from the windows. The low ceiling made the room feel cramped, so instead of ignoring it, we incorporated it into the design by painting it royal blue. Adding cushions to the existing window seat introduced a reading spot, and playful primary colored art was framed and hung to spell "Love Y'all." Now this peppy space is colorful and energetic, and the kids and adults both adore it.

PRICE THIS ROOM

You don't have to spend a lot of money to make a strong visual impact. This room was decorated for around $150!

1 **VINTAGE NFL BANNERS—$33.88** (EBAY)

2 **ANTIQUE BOOKCASE ACCESSORIES—$1–10** EACH (GARAGE SALES) Notice, there is no headboard—the bookshelf acts as the headboard.

3 **CLIP-ON DESK LAMPS—$14** EACH (AMAZON)

4 **BLANKETS—$29.99** EACH (TARGET)

5 **BEDDING—$39.99** (TARGET)

SIX

CELEBRATING STORY

Celebrate Your People

I PUSHED PAST LINED-UP KNEECAPS to squeeze into a seat in the already full church pew. Grief-stricken friends, once banded together with prayers and casseroles, now clutched tissues as they waited for the service for our mutual friend to start. She and I had met in elementary school and had fantastic memories reminiscent of a middle school novel—campouts, Girl Scouts, sleepovers, and times spent toilet-papering the yards of our friends' houses.

During the service, person after person stood at the pulpit to extol their favorite qualities about this young mother of two who left us far too early. A fellow camp counselor commented on her stalwart friendship. A high school confidante explained how she never forgot a birthday and always celebrated with a beautifully wrapped gift. I knew these things about my friend, but as I listened to testimony after testimony, I wondered if she knew just how dearly she was loved. In fact, at each funeral I attend, I have the same thought beating at my skull like a drum line. It almost pains me to hear these loving testimonies, as I fear that we failed our dear one. Sitting at the memorial service of that friend, I once again resolved to do better with people in my life.

TIME IS A FUNNY THING, isn't it? Query one hundred people waiting in line for coffee and most would answer that one of the main purposes of their life boils down to loving their people well. Yet, if we gave away coffee to anyone who expressed that love in a tangible way to a loved one today, we might only see a few free streaming mugs of java. I find myself often so busy with the least important, yet seemingly urgent distractions that, like chucking an airball across the basketball court when the buzzer sounds, I hope my best intentions are magically felt and translated into action. Clearly one "I love you" at the marriage altar is not enough to sustain reaching a golden anniversary. It takes frequent and repeated effort, just as all our relationships do. I contend that one way to bridge the gap and tangibly and frequently demonstrate our care is by delighting in those we love. With this in mind, can we set up our homes to tell our stories in a way that honors and celebrates those who reside there?

Celebrations carry more magnitude than a simple fun factor. Our history books will likely report that we are living in the most connected era of history, yet our reality is we're disconnected in the ways that matter most. It only takes a step outside our front doors to observe couples and families sitting silently next to each other, looking at their phones and ignoring those beside them to interact with people worlds away. Researchers have found this to be such a growing phenomenon—from teenagers to the elderly—that they have actually given it a name: being "alone together."[1] It's no wonder that over three of every five Americans report feeling lonely.[2] In what must be labeled the most depressing research findings in history, British children spend less time playing outdoors than British inmates.[3] Further research found that women on Instagram are more depressed, anxious, and feel less attractive than those without social media accounts.[4] And we've all heard the widespread reports that as teenagers increase their social media usage, they report more depressive tendencies.[5] I don't know about you, but these bleak statistics can feel daunting as I attempt to introduce a more connected alternative to those I love.

Celebration provides a way to slow down, look back, and be grateful.

Amid these sobering truths, research suggests that celebrating with our loved ones *can* make some impact. Studies observing sports teams conclude that the more teams celebrate together, the more likely they are to win. Could that be right? Just commemorating a win together actually leads to climbing numbers on the scoreboard. An examination of basketball games shows a similar outcome. The teams that encouraged each other with taps, fist bumps, hugs, pats, and high-fives had a higher likelihood of winning. These studies clearly teach us that encouraging celebration is not just enjoyable, it's actually beneficial.[6] Another study, this time on marriages, found that spouses who celebrated their partner during good times also *believed* they would be supportive during the bad times.[7] Here is the crazy thing—the spouses didn't have to actually act in an encouraging manner. Just the mere *thought* that the spouse would be supportive, based on past celebrations, increased future intimacy, trust, and satisfaction in the marriage. Basically, if you cheer on your partner's celebrations, you win future relationship points, even without doing anything. Free points, guys. You heard it here first. From this research, it sounds like celebrating together can be the glue that holds relational bonds tight. Giving and receiving hugs reduces stress and results in helping older people maintain health. Even just face-to-face interaction is proven to beat some mental disorders. Talk about simple. All we have to do is show up and we are already investing in our loved ones.[8]

Celebrating matters. But what does it look like to honor the people who we are around most? And what *is* celebrating, really? This concept is more about thoughtfulness than a three-layer cake with candles. Celebration provides a way to slow down, look back, and be grateful. It takes time to notice and join together to acknowledge someone. It can also look like taking ordinary events, such as a Friday night at home, and making them special.

CONNECTION ISN'T COMPLEX

In my family, we observe the end of the school week by ordering pizza. (Sometimes I also celebrate not cooking dinner by ordering pizza.) We've also been known to commemorate a basketball game by getting a treat on the way home—sometimes it's celebration ice cream and sometimes it's consolation ice cream.

In the spirit of self-care, I celebrate my hard work every week by treating myself to a bouquet of fresh flowers on my kitchen table. Often, when I go to the grocery store, I reward myself for doing this difficult adulting task by adding a treat for myself to my cart at the checkout counter. Going to the grocery store is hard, y'all. You deserve a reward for it. Buy that magazine.

In the *Art of Gathering*, an intriguing book that unpacks how to create a meaningful gathering, author Priya Parker argues that today's gatherings are frequently lacking connection, but with conscious effort, we can create it in a meaningful way.[9] To do this practically, we first create a purpose for the event and infuse thoughtfulness in planning details. Would you believe one of the most important places to start is the guest list? Parker argues that who you do *not* invite is just as important as who you do. I know every Southern woman is wringing her hands at the thought of leaving someone out, so here is a simple rule to follow to know who makes the cut: only include guests who add to the purpose of the event. Then, prior to the party, prepare guests on what to expect before they come. When they arrive, as a host committed to connection, you lead them through thoughtful conversation topics, which will aid in bonding.

I was enthralled to read about a group of strangers at an actual dinner party in London in which each course had a new question to ponder and discuss. As the dinner went on, party attendees were encouraged to open up and share. Because I love great food, in dreaming up a similar event of my own, I deviated from the courses Parker listed in her book to include what I would want to eat instead.

For starters, guests answered questions like, "How have your priorities changed over the years?" and "How has your background and experience limited or favored you?" (I envision this as warm brie with apricot jelly and sourdough bread.)

During soups, there was an invitation to ask, "Which parts of your life have been a waste of time?" Um. Ouch. This course is going to be interesting. All of middle school? (At my dinner table, this is a salad—crisp romaine with strawberries, candied pecans, blue cheese, and vinaigrette dressing.)

Under fish, the question of the hour was, "What have you rebelled against in the past and what are you rebelling against now?" (In my house, this is steak or chicken or some delicious pasta.)

Dessert is always my favorite. Because you cannot go wrong with a classic, this course will consist of soft chocolate chip cookies, freshly baked and still warm from the oven, paired with a side of vanilla ice cream. As our eyes roll back in our heads from the deliciousness, we will discuss a question like, "What are the limits of your compassion?"

This is not for the weak, guys. We will be getting deep over some Toll House and Blue Bell. Which, honestly, my soul longs for. These penetrating questions are more interesting and relevant than the current forecast or trending gas prices. By following these guidelines and introducing a purpose to the party, anything from a meeting to a barbecue has the potential to refresh and compel, as well as aid in desperately needed connection. When was the last time you had a work meeting that felt refreshing?

My friend Mary is my real-life example to follow. A natural host, she graciously opens her home with a rotating door of sorts, hosting events throughout the year. I was thrilled to snag an invitation to her Christmas brunch, but aware that I did not know the other attendees, I also felt some party jitters. As I weaved my way through the guests, I made awkward introductions, then busied myself with my phone after conversation ran dry. Once we sat down for lunch behind our personalized name cards at the beautifully set table, it was apparent that small talk was not on the menu. Unknowingly following Parker's best advice, Mary set the stage for

meaningful conversation. She asked us to introduce ourselves and divulge two details: how we knew the host and what wins we experienced in the past year.

Instantly, it was as if Mary gave us the tools to break the dam and loose the connection we all inwardly longed for. Since it is difficult to talk about a win without explaining the loss that occurred first, in this safe place, women were suddenly sharing deep stories of loss, sickness, death, and divorce. Most of us were emotional as we cheered for some and cried with others. As plates were cleared and we savored the last spoonfuls of chocolate crème ganache, I felt as if I was leaving through a completely different room than the one I arrived in. The awkward small talk was gone. Where before we were quietly milling around, we were now exchanging numbers, giving lingering hugs, and exhorting words of encouragement and perseverance. By carefully planning this party with a goal and an agenda, Mary transformed this holiday gathering into something much more significant than sharing a meal. It was now the conduit to connect with the hearts of a dozen other women who had more in common than they realized. I drove away inspired, full of life, and feeling seen and validated. That, my friends, is celebrating people with intention.

INFUSE YOUR HOME WITH A CELEBRATION SPIRIT

So far we have traveled room by room, making the most of the spaces we've discussed and telling our stories through design. I could continue to divulge all the design tips I know, but without this chapter, the most beautifully appointed home could still feel cold and sterile. Though it's placed later in the book, this chapter can provide a foundation for all the others, because I'm going to focus heavily on the spirit of the home, as that is a crucial part of telling your story. Let me introduce you to some ways to have what I call a celebration spirit, which I see as an integral part of the heart of the home.

Treat Family like Strangers

When we commit to celebrating our people, we commit to a mindset shift. Have you noticed that we tend to be more cordial to strangers than to the people we love the most? In public, manners—"thank you" and "excuse me"—are hopefully the standard for most of us, including the awkward jog when someone is holding the door open but you are too far away so you try to fast-walk and say thank you to fill the time. Yet when we get home, we somehow believe our dearest ones are not deserving of the smallest courtesies. There is no awkward jog or thank-you for them.

One way to spark that celebration spirit is to simply consider our words and the tone in which we speak to those closest to us. No doubt, the people we live with often see the worst of us. But if our harsh words are more the rule than the exception, a change is in order. To help this practice come to life, you can pretend a reality show camera is following you around.

Often I don't realize my strong inflection until I have already started talking. I have been guilty of the quick work-around, where I start a sentence with an accidentally-harsher-than-I-meant tone, then I quickly change to cheerfully deliver the last part of the sentence. I count on most people remembering the most recent words they heard, so I hope to Jedi mind trick them into thinking I was speaking kindly the entire time. Does this work? Not really sure, but a course correction is better than no correction at all. My goal is to get to the point where my tone sounds nice all the time and I don't rely on *Star Wars* techniques. It is amazing what we hear when we just start paying attention to how we speak to those we love. And as Mother Teresa once said, if we want to change the world, it starts at home with loving our family.[10]

Appreciate People in Real Time

One phrase that helps me remember how to appreciate others in a practical way is a remark often attributed to Oscar Wilde: "The smallest act of kindness is worth more than the grandest intention." Because, believe me, I have grand intentions. Sending flowers, writing thank-you notes, baking casseroles and cookies, and calling the retail manager to say what a good job their staff is doing at my favorite store—my brain bursts full of wonderful, caring intentions. In my mind, I am the fairy godmother, bibbidi-bobbidi-boo-ing my way through each day, blessing people with my magic wand, and slinging out kindnesses like parade candy. That is, until I get home after a long day or spend more of the day driving in the car than with my feet on solid ground. So many good intentions get lost when I am tired or busy, and as a business owner and mom, that is more often than not.

Following my motto of "the smallest act of kindness is worth more than the grandest intention," when I want to commend a job well done, I just say it, right then and there. No frills. My words might not be paired with a cookie bouquet, but a kind and thoughtful text is better than nothing at all. A lot of times, this looks like simply telling people things in real time.

A small kindness is better than no kindness at all.

When a server waits on the table well, I leave a nice tip and also write an accolade on the receipt for her manager to see when she tallies the money. If someone wants me to pray for them, I pray before we move on to the next conversation. If I appreciate someone's help, I call them and say it. It's not a perfect system, but it is a good one, and that can be enough. After all, a small kindness is better than no kindness at all.

Invest in Toys for a Greater Good

Oh, what's that? Your children voluntarily tell you things? I mean, I heard a rumor that this happens, but just like that mysterious multilevel business my friend runs on Facebook, I don't really understand it. No matter how verbose the child is, I'm convinced at some time in every parent's life, they become an amateur detective, piecing together clues about their child's life as they follow breadcrumb trails. They stand at the metaphorical giant crime board, connecting small facts with yarn secured by pushpins, in hopes of guiding their children to become responsible adults.

Contrary to Amy Poehler's character in *Mean Girls*, I do not care about being the cool mom. I would much rather be an informed mom. Thankfully, I know one way to accomplish it. The answer is to have the "fun house," the house where all the kids want to play.

When everyone hangs out at your house, you know what everyone is doing. You know what they're watching, what they're joking about, and what names they call their friends. Adults can sink into the background as a fly on the wall, overhearing snippets of information while kids eat, joke, eat, play, and eat some more. Because when they do these things, they also talk. So, when information might otherwise be scarce, the puzzle pieces begin to fall in place, and that leads to solving the mystery of "how my child is really doing." Being the parent at the fun house is an investment in stuff that pays off as an investment in relationships.

So, if life and budget allow it, get the foosball table. Turn the extra bedroom into a YouTube studio. Install that NBA-grade basketball hoop in your yard. Buy extra sets of pickleball paddles. Go ahead and go to the warehouse store and get the yearly supply of chips and know that it will be gone before next weekend. Whatever your kids spend their time on, buy two of them. It just might pay off greatly in understanding an older child more than you think, and that holds the value of one thousand Ping-Pong tables.

Find the Wins in Small Details

Celebrating people can go one step further than giving an honored recipient the special plate at dinner or letting them choose the restaurant on their birthday. I love those traditions, but I try to find everyday ways to reinforce how much my kids matter to me. This looks like:

- Hanging a straight-A report card on the refrigerator with "Way to go, Smart-Pants" written on it.
- Documenting important dates on the family calendar to ensure events are attended and seen as valued.
- Taking photos of kids with their friends and making an effort to print and frame them in their room.
- Ensuring kids spend time with their extended family without me around. I want my relatives to know my kids—and that includes who they are without their mom watching over their shoulder. Bonds can be strengthened during ordinary, everyday interactions. One simple way I encourage interaction is when we follow each other in our own cars to meet at the same location, I will often ask my kids to ride with someone else. This small gesture gives my kids time to complain about me with different members of the family.
- Finding creative ways to send them mail. As a kiddo, getting mail rivals hearing the bells of the ice-cream truck. But when they live in your house, this can be a challenge. Getting mail to your child could mean sending them a letter when they go to camp or gifting them a subscription to a children's magazine. When they are spending the night outside of our home, I like sticking a note in their bag for them to find when they unpack. (Side note: when you hear the bell of the ice-cream truck, always buy the ice cream.)

I once overheard someone say they didn't want to give compliments to their loved ones in case it resulted in future arrogance. Y'all, if having a swelled head is the worst of my relatives' problems, I'm gonna go ahead and check that off as "Winning at Life." You already know that our world is filled with violence, division, and angst. We are living through things that make most of us feel pretty beat-up. But with our words alone, we have the awe-inducing power to speak into someone's life and build them up. Real life is already so tiresome—let's wield the power we have for good. If we send out our loved ones with a puffed-up chest, at least they will have some cushion when they come across the blows life will inevitably bring. How they handle our kindnesses is their responsibility. Making the choice to be edifying is ours. Whitney Goodman, LMFT, seconds these thoughts: "As a therapist, I've noticed how we don't tell people we love them . . . as often as we should. It's important to build up your friends, family, and your partner in front of other people and when you are alone. . . . Highlighting the reasons you love someone is good for you, good for the relationship, and good for the other person."[11]

Here are some ways to use your words to encourage your favorite people:

- Create a tradition that honors the birthday guest. Each birthday, take turns around the table and share something you appreciate about the person of honor. Perhaps share a favorite memory to-gether. Create a keepsake by writing down these compliments on a nice piece of cardstock to keep and review the next year. If it is for a child, you could frame the paper, place it in their room, and replace it the next year as a reminder that they are growing and changing.
- On Valentine's Day, cut out red paper hearts, and on each, list something you love about them. Then place the hearts in their home, on the bathroom mirror, in the mail, or on the door of their

room. My kids love this so much that they leave the hearts up for months.

- Take to heart the old adage "praise in public, criticize in private" and find ways to speak well of those you love in front of others. Let them overhear you bragging on them. For kids especially, instead of talking about physical appearances—a go-to topic of conversation among adults for some strange reason (*He's getting so big! She looks so pretty!*)—brag about things they have control over, such as good decisions they made or ways they are persevering to accomplish a goal. Praise the things you want to see more of. If your loved ones are receptive to being praised in front of others, take advantage of that while you are in front of them, so they hear evidence of positive things you say behind their back.

- Since I alluded to this already, can I put on my parent hat for a second? I realize that commenting on a child's physical appearance is often done with innocent intent; however, our kids hear these comments repeatedly and remember them. Sometimes they allow our words to become part of the story they tell themselves. In fact, research proves this kind of praise is actually a detriment, and it's more helpful to give attention to things like hard work, effort, and strategy.[12]

Occasionally I do not know how to engage someone, so I might grab on to the lowest hanging fruit and pay them a seemingly innocent compliment about their appearance. As adults, I hope we know better than to say words to children that may take root in their already insecure hearts, no matter how innocent those words seem. The reality is, when they interact with other kids, they are hearing messages about their appearance all the time. We are just another voice in the crowd. I have watched as my friends' kids have struggled with normal physical features but feel self-conscious because it's been pointed out so often. Things as simple as being tall can feel like a label, and most people don't like to be labeled because none of us are just one thing. As adults who love and care, by praising attributes other than their appearance, which most kids have no control over anyway, we provide a model to follow and reinforce character qualities to continue. I invite you to go deeper than surface level when you interact with all people, but especially those who are still forming their self-worth. Parenting hat removed.

Create Your Own Holiday

In my last years of college, my classes were demanding. Graduating a semester early caused an even heftier course load, and the pressure was real. My study friend and I realized we needed a break, so we invented a mini holiday by celebrating the first of every month. Being broke college kids, we commemorated the moment in the most extravagant manner we could dream up—ordering dessert at a restaurant! We might as well have had a five-course meal at the Ritz for how special it felt to get away from campus and splurge. We talked and laughed and, most of all, looked forward to the next first day of the month so we could do it all again.

Another funny friend observed that it never really felt like Christmas until two weeks into the month. She reasoned that the first part of December flew by in a chaotic flash, but by the fourteenth, lights hung in trees, carols played on the radio, and magic filled the air. This random observation made me laugh at first, then I saw a little truth in it. From then on, we would get together to celebrate this random day in the last month of the year. It has been twenty years and multiple kids later, but we still wish each other a happy December 14 every year. Every time I reach out, she tells me how thrilled she feels that I remember our special day.

What random day can you celebrate? The first of the month? Your pet's birthday? The day you met your best friend? Payday? The seventeenth of the month because it is your lucky number? Choose an ordinary day to turn into your own personal holiday and celebrate it with someone you love.

PUT THE FUN IN MUNDANE

I have an extremely weighty job as the matriarch of the family. I liken it back to the days when women wore corsets and had dance cards and men were under considerable pressure to carry on the family name. This burden on my shoulders comes from my self-appointed role as Family Fun Ambassador, and, friends, it is no small role. My job description has requirements like arguing that "movie nights are fun" and "Christmas lights are not boring" and "family time is important" and "eat at the table, not in your room." You get the point. My kids can turn almost anything into a battle, and I am wearing my dress blues.

As the Family Fun Ambassador, I am prowling along my family's lives, waiting to overhear any life snippet that needs to be transformed into a memory. Remember how we discussed that photos aid our memories? I make sure we also take a photo of said memories to ensure they aren't forgotten. You better believe my boys have scrapbooks filled with photos of us together at school parties and eating in the cafeteria. It never hurts to have a little hard evidence that I was an attentive mom. When I realized my nephews had no recollection of the grueling weekends I spent baking in the Texas sun as I cheered on their baseball games, I decided I needed a physical backup in the yearly scrapbook with my own offspring in case their memories waned.

Recently, when a new opportunity came across my desk, I faced a rare dilemma. Part of being the Fun Ambassador means that I unearth celebration moments for others, but this time, the tomfoolery was knocking on my door. Could I pass up a memorable opportunity to show my kids how we celebrate others by celebrating . . . *myself*? I needed to consult the experts.

When I attended the fun academy to earn my ambassadorship, I learned how to deal with the hand you are given and how to make it fun. The motto is WWBGD, which, of course, stands for *What Would Bob Goff Do?* Bob Goff is a bestselling author with more whimsy in his pinky than I could hope to gather over a lifetime. I want to be him when I grow up. So, when this interesting opportunity landed on my desk, I straightened my beret, pulled up my knee socks, and prepared myself to lead by example. I planned a goodbye party for my gallbladder.

Yes, you read that right. I never thought I would write those words in the same sentence, and I likely never will again. When a persistent pain in my side revealed itself to be gallstones, the only solution was to remove my gallbladder. The whole darn thing. This felt momentous. After all, this organ served me well for multiple decades, and now it was leaving for the big gallbladder in the sky. I think losing an organ deserves a party, and every party needs a cake. So, naturally, I set about ordering a goodbye cake for my gallbladder.

The first hurdle was actually ordering the cake. I held in hysterical tears of laughter when I attempted to explain my needs at the local bakery. In fact, the first location refused to help me. Bless their hearts. Ripping off the gallbladder Band-Aid did not work the first time, so obviously I needed to change my ordering tactics. On my second bakery phone call, I decided to be coy. I did not want to scare them away, so I attempted to ease it into the conversation nonchalantly.

"Yes, I would like an eight-inch round, strawberry cake . . . turquoise icing with kelly green accents. And can you write 'Gone but not forgotten' on it?"

Pause.

Breathe in.

Pause.

In the most casual tone I could muster, I asked, "Also, do you happen to know what a gallbladder looks like?" And then, mumbling under my breath a little too fast, I asked, "Can you draw a pink one with a happy face?"

Another pause.

When my youngest son and I picked up the cake, we lifted the bakery box lid with anticipation, then erupted with laughter. The baker captured exactly what I hoped for, and that happy gallbladder turned out pretty stinking adorable. I tracked down the cake artist to tell her how delighted we were (see: praising people in real time), then set out to say goodbye to my faithful organ.

The next week, I learned that my best friend would soon undergo a similar surgery. With the unusual cake order fresh in my mind, I realized my own party was simply the pregame for celebrating her. Plus, now I knew what to say to successfully order such a weird cake and not confuse the bakery. When my friend gingerly toddled to the door after surgery to see our shining faces holding a bundle of flowers and a quirky cake, an enormous grin covered her entire face. I know she felt all the love and prayers I intended when I handed her that mix of flour and sugar topped with a smiling gallbladder.

For being so simple, the benefits of celebrating our people are far-reaching. Sometimes a kind gesture truly makes the difference between hope and despair.

We really do need each other. We need people who will let someone over in traffic, even when they tried to skip the line we all waited in. We need a friend who notices when we miss a meeting and texts to check if things are okay. We need the person who remembers our birthday, even when we forgot theirs. We need someone to sit in our grief with us and not try to comfort us with optimistic platitudes but respond with validation and acknowledgment of loss. Some days, simply listening can be so much more meaningful than spouting trite advice. And we need to do it.

It just might be that a small kindness will encourage someone on the day they need it most, the day that is bigger than they can bear. We truly have no idea what people are facing in their inner lives, but we have the opportunity to give a glimmer of hope.

During a recent relocation, I noticed one of the movers I hired was quite prickly with the others, answering in short clips and rolling his eyes at them. Later that day, he said he saw something about our family that encouraged him, and the once-brusque mover confided that he had been diagnosed with brain cancer and was fighting a tough battle. This broad, muscular man's eyes filled with tears as he described his struggle. After sharing his story and receiving our encouragement and prayers, he was noticeably changed. He led the way for the crew, tackling each task more chipper than Mary Poppins on her arrival day. I believe that by celebrating our people and the people around us, we can encourage those who need it and, one by one, we can change the world.

SIX WAYS TO CELEBRATE YOUR PEOPLE

Once you begin to look for opportunities to celebrate, you will find them everywhere. These are some of my favorite ways to make small things seem big to celebrate my people.[13]

Wacky Dinner

Take some family members or friends to the grocery store and let them pick out anything they want for dinner—even candy, chips, etc. This is especially fun when you bring kids. It will be hilarious to see what each person chooses. Jar of pickles? Okay. Tootsie rolls? Sure. Can of stinky sardines? Umm, maybe. Anything goes!

Play Hooky

Occasionally my parents allowed me to skip school as a kid. One day in my junior year, when a large semester project loomed over my head, I stayed home from school and enjoyed the beautiful spring day outdoors. I returned to school the next morning rested, recharged, and ready to conquer my big assignment. It was eye-opening to learn my absence didn't make me fall behind, as I assumed it would, but instead gave me a break to gather momentum to face my task. I typically handled big assignments by working tirelessly, like I would win a prize if I did not take a break. This helpful lesson taught me that allowing myself to take a break actually helped me feel more prepared.

How can you facilitate letting a loved one off the hook? Maybe your spouse makes the same annoying mistake for the fourth time, and instead of mentioning it, you keep it to yourself. Maybe you pick up an extra liter of your roommate's favorite drink to save them a trip to the store. Maybe you give all your employees an extra casual day or work-from-home day. Maybe you need to give grace to yourself and take a mental health day to sleep a few extra hours. We all need a break, and we reinforce our love when we let those we care about have some grace and maybe even play hooky.

Delightful Bait and Switch

The premise of this treat is to plan for one situation, then surprise someone with an unexpected treat. One fun idea to try with kids is to commence with the bedtime ritual just like every night—brush teeth, put pj's on, and tuck them in. Before they fall asleep, get them up and inform them you are all going on a donut or ice cream run instead of sleeping. Take a trip, including the pj's, and enjoy a late-night snack together.

You might not have a child to wake up and treat, but anyone can expect one plan and be surprised when something delightful happens instead. Could you fake a boring meeting or errand and then drive someone to their favorite restaurant or even a live concert? How can you set a plan for the mundane and reveal an unexpected, delightful alternative?

Pass-Along Journal

In college, my roommates were lovely women from all across the nation. We once shared blue boxes of macaroni and cheese and binge-watched the Olympics, and after college we all moved back to our respective states, vowing to get together once a year. On one of our post-college trips, we bought a gorgeous leather-bound journal and wrote a summary of our trip together. The Pass-Along Journal was born. Each person gets it to write a summary of the year, post photos, and share news, then when we reconvene the next year, we review it and pass it to the next friend. When we started this journal, we didn't realize we were creating a tangible way to document what has happened over twenty years of memories, and even better, twenty years of hairstyles.

The Shirt of the Year

Memorialize an outfit you wore for a significant life event, such as when you got engaged. One friend references the shirt her husband wore during the proposal as the "shirt of the year" every time he wears it again. This nickname pays playful homage to how important that day became in the story of their family. Designate a special article of clothing as the new honored item. Light a candle and hold a ridiculously solemn ceremony to announce its new status.

Grown-Up Scavenger Hunt

Texas is big. It's not uncommon for us to drive thirty minutes to an hour to meet someone. Such was the case with a colleague who lived an hour away. I made the drive to her and, knowing she would drive the same highway to make the trek in the next few days to me, I wanted to hide something along her route. I found an extremely obscure area of a gas station and hid a coupon for coffee under a statue. The next week before she started the drive to me, I texted her a photo of the hiding place and the location and told her if she could find the coupon, that morning's coffee

was on me. This unexpected treasure hunt put a punch of energy and fun into the work we shared and left her laughing for days.

Will you be passing through the same place as a loved one? Find a hiding place that is unlikely to be discovered and something fun to leave that is not too valuable. Then create the clues and let the game begin.

TELL YOUR STORY THROUGH CHERISHED MEMORIES

Celebrating loved ones through design has been a core tenet of my design aesthetic for years now. Remember the comments a fellow contestant on that reality show made about my use of family photos and the lack of art?

Though it stung at the time, she was accurate. I use family photos because the art I adore is made up of the faces of the people I love. I want to surround myself with happy memories.

These are some of my favorite ways to tell my story through design.

Watercolor (or Commission) the Exterior of Your First or Favorite House

When my house was included on a historic home tour, an artist sat outside and painted a watercolor as the tour took place. After the weekend, we were gifted this beautiful piece of art. I treasured it so much that I began to give my design clients a similar gift. If you love the house you're in, consider commissioning a custom painting as a unique way to commemorate it.

Frame Special Mementos from Birth and Childhood

We covered this extensively in the last chapter, so this is a reminder: Childhood gives us precious keepsakes worth framing. In my home, I have a large shadow box with the outfits my two boys wore home from the hospital, complete with tiny hats and miniature booties. Similarly, one of my clients had several dresses from her daughter's childhood, now vintage. We found pretty hangers and hung them as a collection on the wall. Other ideas for items to frame are shoes, a first lock of hair, hospital wristbands or onesies, newspaper clips or coins from the day a child was born, their adoption decree, or the court photo from the day the adoption was finalized.

What do you do with your childhood toys? I put a special few in my kids' rooms and the rest sit in my drafty attic because I do not know what to do with them. I was delighted when I walked into my older sister's closet and saw how she creatively solved her toy dilemma. A natural-born nurturer, she loved dolls growing up. In fact, so many years later, she still talks about some of her favorites from her childhood. She gathered a few of them and displayed them on an unused shelf in her closet. This sweet celebration of her childhood is like a hidden Easter egg that only she sees, and it makes her happy each morning.

Commemorate the Big Day

Are sacred wedding mementos gathering dust in your attic? I love freeing those gorgeous wedding heels from that stuffy box and showcasing them under a large glass cloche. Perhaps you could frame your ring pillow and a ribbon from your bouquet. Keep those vows front and center by displaying these sweet mementos of such a special day. A wedding isn't the only big day to celebrate. You can easily frame a graduation cap or degree.

Celebrate a Goal or Event

Some people run only when someone is chasing them, and apparently others train and run entire marathons just for fun! Did you have an amazing adventure or accomplish a challenging goal? Display a memento from that occasion. Ideas include travel postcards, maps, metro cards, coins, Mickey Mouse ears, or awards (such as a marathon medal).

A few years ago, I had the opportunity to go on an adventure I had longed to be a part of for years. Tickets to *Saturday Night Live* are almost impossible to get and after nearly a decade of trying, I won them from the NBC lottery. It felt surreal to stand in the studio of a show I watched growing up, observing how small the set looked in comparison to how it looked on TV. I ambled down the back hall, gawking at the photos of decades of hosts, pinching myself knowing Steve Martin walked along the very same ground. I lingered in the backstage area, attempting to act unaffected when I spied current cast members. I loitered so long that the NBC page had to shoo me out. Needless to say, I framed the wristband from that experience with photos from that momentous night, and they help me remember the magic I felt.

For a budding young golfing client, I hung all his medals from a long shelf and put his trophies on top. This is a simple way to display awards, and best of all, it transports them out of storage boxes under the bed.

I would not be a true Texan if I did not decorate for a modern-day cowboy. Part of finishing out this client's living room was finding a creative way to display his rodeo awards. Do you know what they give for a prize when you win a rodeo? Not a trophy. Not a ribbon. Not in Texas. I had no idea they actually give belt buckles as a prize! To feature these, a glass-top table with a wide base acted as a display case where we placed his trophy buckles and thus included them as a part of his story.

Combine Well-Loved T-Shirts into a Quilt

Like the tree falling in the forest with no one to hear it, in college, if there was not a T-shirt to commemorate an event, did it even happen? I loved collecting shirts for every event, and though I don't wear them these days, seeing them reminds me of happy memories. You may savor shirts from a baseball team, cheer tournament, or church youth group. Transforming these into a blanket is a fun way to turn those memories into something useful.

A FRIEND RECENTLY TOLD ME about a memorial service he planned for a dear comrade named Carl. He originally met Carl in a vintage car and scooter aficionado group, and they shared a love for anything automotive. At Carl's funeral service, people met at Carl's favorite pub and had Carl's favorite drink in his honor. They then held a scooter parade and headed to another location where they all participated in a scooter obstacle course. They spent the evening together, reminiscing and telling stories about their dear friend. Now every year at their annual get-together, they have the Carl Memorial Shenanigans Award, which is simply a glass and matchbook from Carl's favorite restaurant, Panchos.

The instant I heard this, I wanted to meet Carl, then hug my friend, then join his group of friends. What a creative, fantastic celebration of life. By hearing this story, I got a real sense of who Carl was and how dearly loved he was by those who knew him best. Isn't that what life should be? Taking the time to celebrate one another and demonstrate our love and appreciation for one another. It makes me wonder if we have to keep our outdated rituals.

What if we truly honored and celebrated our loved ones before they are gone? A recent Twitter post went viral when the author mused, "Everything we say at funerals should be said at birthday parties instead. We leave so much love unspoken."[14] What if our best party to celebrate someone was actually their birthday, not their funeral? Many people minimize birthdays and treat them like just another day. And sometimes it is. But for a loved one with a big milestone birthday, could we lavishly celebrate them? Could we speak well of them, tell their funny stories, and instead of going all out on their funeral, could we go all out on their life? Isn't it logical that the party we have when they are alive should at least rival the memorial we give them in death? I am determined to do better and love people more while they are alive.

As I leave you with ideas to celebrate your people while telling their story, I want to remind you that our days are numbered. This is not said with a doom-and-gloom, tinfoil hat voice, but with a healthy perspective that the only day any of us is promised is today. Is there someone who needs to hear how much they really mean to you? Relationships can be so complex, and it's amazing what a heartfelt compliment can mean. Author Donald Miller said when we die, strangers will be talking about what we built, but our loved ones will talk about the way we did (or did not) build them up.[15] Let today be the day you send that text, write that note, or make that call.

I'm taking my own advice. My mom's birthday is nearing, and when I thought about hosting a party for her, I quickly dismissed the idea because her age is not one that is normally associated with celebration. It's just a random birthday. However, I realized when your age begins with a seven, every birthday is a milestone. I value this woman so much that I moved my family an hour closer to her last year, wanting to give my children a chance to know and enjoy more of my extended family. If I would go to such extremes, why would I wait for the next round number to celebrate her?

Because there is no time like the present, and I don't need an occasion to celebrate the lady who brought me into the world, I am already planning a big party in her honor. Even if her birthday does not end in zero or five. As goes the humor in my family, I am sure she will think that we're having a party for her because we think she is going to die this year. But the truth is, I don't know what is going to happen to any of my loved ones tomorrow, but I can do something special today. So I will.

Now it's your turn. Who in your life needs to be celebrated? What can you do today to make that happen? How can you use your words and life to invest in the story they tell themselves they are worthy of celebrating?

ACTION STEPS

TO CELEBRATE YOUR PEOPLE

After discussing the benefits of celebrating your people, consider one way to incorporate celebration in your own circles this week.

Ideas to consider:

- host a Friday night celebration
- weigh your words (speak as kind to your loved ones as you do to strangers)
- thank people in real time
- choose-your-own-dinner night
- play hooky together
- surprise someone you love with an unplanned treat run
- start a journal to document a meaningful relationship
- designate a shirt of the year
- invest in toys your family loves for a greater good
- speak well of someone behind their back and in front of others

- celebrate small wins
- invent your own holiday
- notice and check in when someone seems sad
- create your own travel scavenger hunt
- commission a first home/favorite home watercolor
- frame a childhood memento and commemorate a special day
- celebrate an accomplished goal or an award
- plan a party for someone you love

And those are just for starters. Review the chapter for many more ideas or invent your own that fit your story best.

This oversized landing was screaming for reassignment. The space turned into a landing spot for a smattering of random toys, and this mom of four knew there was a much better use. No re-painting was needed—because if it's not broke, we don't fix it. Instead, the existing gray paint provided a cohesive backdrop for three identical chalkboards with vinyl lettering under three indus-trial pendant lamps. A remnant from another project provided enough wood for a free-floating desk, and three coordinating chairs are pulled up to encourage homework tackling.

HOW TO WELCOME GUESTS INTO YOUR HOME

The True Art of Hospitality

A natural by-product of gratitude is sharing with others, so an overflow of a thankful heart for our home results in hospitality. Yet, how do we ensure that we are gracious hosts and don't regard our guests in the way of Benjamin Franklin who famously said that houseguests, like fish, begin to smell after three days?

I think of thoughtful women who have hosted me. One friend, Nevette, leaves a hydrangea, plucked fresh from her garden, in my room every time I sleep over. Aimee provides a chilled water bottle, a towel, and a fresh box of unopened soap.

Shannon serves homemade chocolate chip cookies, warm from the oven, with a glass of milk. Melissa makes sure to have my favorite drink, Diet Dr Pepper, cooling in the fridge. I remember these visits, not because of the items served, but rather the thoughtfulness behind the gestures.

There is something extraordinary about being treated kindly as a guest. As an adult there are few opportunities to truly serve and care for a friend. Hosting a visitor in our home provides the rare opportunity to tangibly show lavish love. We just discussed the importance of celebrating the people we love. Opening our homes to a guest is perhaps one of the most personal ways to do that.

By including thoughtful touches for them, we say:

I am glad you are here.

You are valued.

I hope you come back.

It is easy to forget how privileged we are to live in a dwelling that has room to host others. When we consider the arrangements of many families in other countries, a home considered small in most of the US would be considered a palace across the world. Because of this, I see opening my home to others as a natural outpouring of a grateful heart. I acknowledge that I have been given more than I deserve, and I would like to share it with others when they have a need. So, how can we do this in a way that honors the guest and serves both parties?

COMMUNICATE CLEARLY UPON ARRIVAL

First things first, upon their arrival in your home, offer guests a drink and, even better, a snack if you have one. (Traveling always makes me hungry.) If you have not asked beforehand, this is a good time to inquire about any dietary restrictions or allergies.

Then share the rules of the house. Is there an area that is off-limits or something they cannot touch? Can kids eat or drink in the living room? Do you prefer they remove their shoes? If this is your rule, a thoughtful gesture is to lend comfy house shoes or soft socks as an alternative. If they are anything like me most of the time, their socks don't match or, worse, have a hole. When you offer an option that keeps their feet toasty, you will win one thousand friendship points and spare them the sock shame they already feel.

Next, let them know the schedule and other important things. For instance, when meals are served, other life obligations you need to attend during their visit, and where snacks and drinks are should they get hungry at 3:00 a.m.

SPOIL THEM WITH EXTRAS AND TREATS

When a friend stays overnight, opportunities to be hospitable open up widely. I stash extra toothbrushes on hand so I can talk my besties into shirking their home responsibilities and crashing with me for a week. Or at least another night.

Of course, snacks, water, and extra blankets are always a nice touch. My friend who owns a vacation rental home surveys her guests when they are booking and has their favorite drink and snack waiting for them upon arrival. Another consideration is to list the Wi-Fi code in the guest room. Want more bonus friendship points? Keep an extra phone charger on hand. That is any traveling teenager's love language, and adults find it pretty useful as well. Some savvy host families provide a welcome basket upon arrival, stuffed with local foodie favorites. Printing out a weather forecast for the week and displaying it can be an appreciated detail. Stock the bathroom with things they may need: shampoo, conditioner, makeup remover, washcloths, mouthwash, lotion, extra toilet paper, air fresheners, and even an iron.

CHANNEL YOUR INNER TRAVEL GUIDE

If you play host to travelers unfamiliar with the area, provide a list of your favorite restaurants and can't-miss coffee shops, as well as parks or other area attractions. Stash a list on your computer and print it out when the next guest arrives. Just like a swanky hotel, leave a copy of your state or regional magazine on the bedside table. Plan a few events while they are there but also give them plenty of free time. When I am a guest, I like to have a little freedom to enter vacation mode, don't you?

BE AVAILABLE

These generous touches will likely help your visitors feel welcomed, yet you must not overlook one of the most important factors in opening your home to others: be available to your guests. I am not suggesting that normal life completely screech to a halt when a newcomer makes an appearance, but rather suggesting that when you are spending time with them, you are present. The phone is put away and you are making eye contact and listening when they talk. It would be a shame to spend so much time cooking or cleaning that you miss out on the actual visit.

It can be challenging to open your home when you feel ashamed or embarrassed by it, so when you invest in your space and use it for others, you actually invest in your relationships. The next time the need arises for a baby shower, community group gathering, or school meeting, I hope you have enough pride in your home to volunteer. Anyone with a credit card can have a beautiful home, but a home open to serve and love others has a different kind of beauty—the kind I strive for my home to embody.

Sometimes hospitality looks like:

- a welcome basket with local favorites
- a small gift upon arrival
- a kitchen stocked with their favorite drinks and snacks
- a local map with recommendations of area attractions and suggestions of can't-miss locales
- communication about the expectations of the home and times of meals
- Wi-Fi code and an extra phone charger
- fresh flowers on the counter
- water bottles in the bedroom
- extra blankets and socks
- space and time to be quiet
- favorite books on the bedside table
- a new toothbrush and bar of soap

SEVEN

MERRYMAKING STORY

Create Christmas Magic

AS WE WERE SITTING AT THE FAMILY BIRTHDAY PARTY, all eyes turned to my mom as she pulled a mysterious item from the bag hanging on her arm. My puzzlement turned to elation as she looked in my direction and explained that these handmade Christmas place mats were crocheted by Elsie, the grandmother I hardly knew.

I come from a line of German farmers. It's quite humorous, actually, because I am the least agricultural type of gal, but such is ancestry. My great-grandparents migrated from Germany and of all the places in these great United States, they settled in North Dakota. I've given a lot of thought as to why they might have settled in a place so frigid. The only reason I can arrive at is perhaps North Dakota is warmer than Germany, so they thought they found paradise? Thankfully, Dad left the frigid winters of the North for graduate school in Texas, and once he experienced Texas hospitality and fifty-degree winters, he never looked back. Unfortunately, living on opposite ends of the country meant that we rarely saw his side of the family, including his mom, Grandma Elsie.

The rest of the family oohed and aahed as I gingerly examined these handmade heirlooms. My mind raced, thrilled with this small inheritance. I didn't know my dad's mom well, and one of the few details I know about her is that she loved to crochet. As I lovingly turned the place mats over to examine the amazing artisanship, I laughed out loud because I saw something that indicated my mom hadn't fully vetted the historical accuracy of her gift.

I CAN ONLY ASSUME what I inherited from my dad's extended side of the family, but the genetic gifts my mom bestowed to me are glaringly obvious. One of the things I am most grateful for is my mother's fantastic sense of humor. Her lightning-fast wit is gift enough, yet this confident lady sits comfortably in her own skin, which enables her to laugh at herself. Humor and maturity can be powerful when paired together, and because I have seen my mother demonstrate them well, I have learned the immeasurable gift of being able to laugh at myself. I giggle when thinking back to a lunch date when she saw a man in uniform and, ever the patriot, approached his table and thanked him for his brave service. It was only after we left the restaurant and passed his truck in the parking lot that I realized she had gotten things a bit wrong. Based on his regalia, she made a natural assumption that he served in the armed forces. However, many jobs require a uniform . . . including the city government. Our brave soldier was actually an animal control worker. I'm sure he never felt so appreciated for catching stray dogs.

But my favorite memory of my mom might be our foray into Warby Parker to buy her a new pair of frames. Any four-eyes knows that buying glasses takes patience, as you try on dozens of pairs before you find the ones that instantly make you look ten years younger. As my dear mother tried on frame after frame, her hands got full, and she absently placed her current pair of glasses down on the shelf among the samples. Unfortunately, once hundreds of frames of glasses are all lined together, it can be difficult to

I see tradition and holiday decor as an indication of a healthy home.

determine where you left yours. At least, if you are my mom. So, in *Where's Waldo?* fashion, we examined each pair, one by one, parsing through the haystack to find that tiny needle, only now shaped like frames. My family spends as much time laughing with Mom as we spend laughing at her, and she joins in, knowing we only laugh because we love her.

I'm sharing stories about my mom for two reasons. First, to follow my own advice and celebrate my people. Not to mention, parents can be extremely entertaining. But the second reason is that growing up, she had an amazing way of making things special, sometimes even inadvertently.

Her occasional forgetfulness benefited her three children most around Christmas. For instance, like most moms, she would hide gifts around the house to avoid peeping eyes (I am looking at you, sister dear). Yet, in the bustle of life, Mom would often forget where she hid the gifts. This meant that some years, on a random Tuesday in February, I would receive a present for no discernible reason. One afternoon after high school dance practice, I remember watching her retrieve a fully wrapped gift with a fluffy bow from the top of the laundry room refrigerator. I do not recall the gift, but I fondly remember how joyous it felt to receive an unexpected surprise. Those forgotten Christmas gifts appeared so frequently that I even began to inwardly hope to get a gift later, perhaps something forgotten behind the dirty laundry basket or under the boxes in the garage. (In my current house, I could hide a gift in the oven, for how much it gets used.)

Last year I longed to make the holiday season memorable for my kids. It has been a year of big changes, and a little fairy dust—or bribery—never hurts when times seem tough. As it usually does, December flew by and, between shopping for family and helping clients decorate for Christmas, a few of my gifts arrived right under the wire on December 23. As soon as I considered placing them under the tree, I envisioned my mom removing that wrapped gift off the top of the laundry room fridge. I don't remember what the box held for me that day—probably a Kaboodle kit or a Debbie Gibson tape— but I recall how exciting it was to get a gift out of nowhere. So, I wrapped the gifts for my boys as usual, then stashed them away in the back of my car.

On the way home from the final Christmas celebrations of the day, when the car sat silent in the afterglow of the holiday, I casually mentioned that I had one more small gift for each of them. I watched their eyes light up, crinkling with excitement at the edges. The items they opened in those boxes were not the best or most expensive gifts they received, but because of the thoughtful presentation, I know that experience of "one more gift" will be one they remember.

As we discussed in chapter 5, there is no other time as special as child-hood. For just a few years, magic fills the air, and as grown-ups, we hold the unique opportunity to harness and cultivate the magic. Current research confirms that there is no time like the present for children. Do you know that creativity declines with age? Kids are inherently skilled at innovative problem solving, and that creativity declines as we learn the rules of how things are "supposed" to be.[1] There is a short window for kids when any-thing is possible. I want to take advantage of that opportunity to create a soft memory so when the hardness of the world comes—and it will—they can face it knowing how loved they are.

I am certainly not advocating for being a supermom.

I am not even almost a supermom.

Most days I am a "just doing my best" mom.

I observe other moms momming so hard, and I admire them. I adore watching friends' antics on social media, especially seeing the creativity of the nightly elves that visit every Christmas. Oddly in our house, much like our Tooth Fairy, our elf forgets to move some nights. Regarding the Tooth Fairy, I knew the jig was up one year when my son texted me saying, "I am not sure the Tooth Fairy is real because she forgot my tooth and left no money." You better bet the Tooth Fairy wrote an apology note and left a bigger bill than she normally would have. We've already established I am not above a bribe. But honestly, guys, the Tooth Fairy is dog-tired. She is no longer skilled at jobs that clock in at midnight. That used to fly when she was a younger tooth sprite, but these days, this fairy needs her sleep. In fact, she told me she usually collapses around nine watching Netflix with the Easter Bunny.

All jokes aside, I see tradition and holiday decor as an indication of a healthy home. This is certainly true as I look back on my adolescence. Al-though I never thought to verbalize it at the time, I delighted in the holiday decor sprinkled throughout the house growing up. I vividly recall admiring our holiday decorations as a child, and deep down I knew that if we had margin to decorate, everything must have been okay. Because, in a crisis, frivolous decor would be the first to go. Holiday decor became an indication that things were harmonious in our house and thus it was a good place to be.

I want to create that warm, stable, special feeling in my home as my kids grow up, complete with traditions they will remember fondly into their adult lives. I'm not advocating for tasks that require upkeep, skilled memory, or nocturnal disposition. Parents don't need one more thing to feel guilty about. Most parents I know feel guilty for it all, and then they feel guilty for feeling guilty. I will be the last person to tell you to "enjoy it while your kids are young" or "don't ever look at your phone." I'm convinced that the people preaching ideas like this are far removed from the daily struggle it is to be a parent of a toddler. I could not have squeezed any more enjoyment from when my kids were babies, but I can also tell you that it was one of the hardest times of my life. My heart goes out to mamas and papas of little ones. The isolation, exhaustion, and mental fatigue from anticipating the next crisis and being on high alert at all times cannot be rivaled. If it keeps you sane to look at your phone for a second, you go right ahead. If you miss your baby's first step, they will take another one. (Just kidding. You should probably pay attention when your kid starts walking.) But really, I'm not here to add anything else to your list of "shoulds." You're already doing a fantastic job just as you are. I simply believe we can do things we are already doing, but with 2 percent more thoughtfulness.

TRADITION TELLS A STORY

What is a tradition? For our purposes, it's basically the same thing done at the same time each year. Meg Cox, the author of *The Book of New Family Traditions*, defines family ritual as "any activity you purposefully repeat together as a family that includes heightened attentiveness and something extra that lifts it above the ordinary ruts."[2]

You don't know how many times I have heard my clients describe what a chore it is to decorate, and some people, especially empty nesters, confide that they don't decorate their home for Christmas at all. Not even with a

little tree. They just didn't see the point. To help all the humbugs out there, here are some of my favorite reasons that traditions matter for all ages.

To Instill That We Are Part of a Bigger Family

A recent study surveyed 1,500 children and concluded those with a high level of grandparental involvement had fewer emotional and behavioral problems.[3] The holidays are prime time for this type of involvement, as this is the most likely time of year that relatives gather. For some geographically disconnected families, the holidays are the only occasion for a reunion all year. Christmas is an opportune time for children of all ages to sit at the feet of their grandparents or extended family members and spend time learning that they are part of a family and thus part of a bigger story. Are you a grandparent? Make an effort to spend as much time with your grandchildren as possible. They need it as much as you do. Do you have nieces or nephews or little cousins? Make the extra effort to be a good role model. Are you a parent of young ones? Incorporate your extended family in your activities. Your kids will benefit greatly.

To Create Security

Kids thrive on routine. Consistency helps life make sense as they feel safe and know what to expect. I certainly understand that. As an adult, I'm in control of what I am doing 100 percent of the day. If I decide I want to change my plans, I am the captain of my own ship. But children move from commitment to commitment, not knowing what is coming next and how to prepare for it. By doing the same thing in the same way at the same time, we gift them stability and an expectation of what to look forward to.

To Create Memories We'll Cherish

Some of my favorite memories are the rituals we engaged in growing up—and because it's my family, those rituals often involved food. Since my dad was the son of German farmers who ate some weird stuff, we also ate some weird stuff. Remember how the Grinch ate roast beast? Our Christmas dinner looked similar. We baked our ham with the bread dough wrapped around the entire piece of meat. It looked like a big hunk of raw dough as it went into the oven, then it came out with the juices from the ham baked into the crispy bread, which we then broke off pieces of and ate.

On my dad's birthday we would have another German dish called Nifla, which is made of hamburger, potatoes, and dumplings. The tradition was twofold—first we ate Nifla and second we complained about eating Nifla. Us kids were unified in our distaste for this unique German dish, and yet even our dislike is a sweet memory to recall.

CREATING YOUR STORY THROUGH CHRISTMAS DECOR

Another fascinating survey of children asked them what they will remember most about childhood. The answers were surprisingly unglamorous. The children listed simple, everyday traditions, like family dinners, holiday get-togethers, and bedtime stories.[4]

As always, as a "doing your best" parent, choose one activity from the list to try this year and tuck away the rest for later. While many of the following ideas are for decor in the home, it is crucial to remember a home is much more than a place with a roof. So, in this chapter, some of the suggestions I am recommending will encourage the *spirit* of telling your story and how to help others tell their story in this meaningful season of giving back.

First of all, let's talk basics. Christmas decor can be as varied as a barista's misspellings of your name. The good news is there are a few rules of thumb that can help you as you decide how to decorate for the holidays.

Embrace Your Christmas Color Scheme

Christmas red and green. They go together like cake and ice cream, getting sleepy after eating turkey and green bean casserole with those crunchy noodles on top on Thanksgiving.

Christmas red and green. They go together like
cake and ice cream.

But what if red and green don't match your room? Is it okay to venture out of the holiday-approved colors and decorate with something different? I am here to tell you it is not only okay, sometimes it is a breath of fresh air. My main tree is NOT red and green. Past-year trees have been black, white, and metallic. Last year I reinvented my look by using peacock blue, pink, and silver.

However, some things are just classics. Though my main tree is not red and green, my entire kitchen is, because something about the classic colors feels festive and cheery for me.

So, where does this leave us? I've got two answers for you.

1. *Please know it is okay if your Christmas decor does not "match" the rest of your house.* Everyone knows it's Christmas. No one is confused why you're using red in an otherwise neutral home. At the holidays, you get a decorating hall pass. Anything goes. For some personality types, this is all you need to hear. You love the classic colors of Christmas and will embrace them wholeheartedly. Still others of us match the color of the kitchen notepad to the paint on the walls, and we want our trees to match the normal decor of our homes. Both are wonderful.

2. *The answer to this question is like that of the TV in the bedroom—there is no right answer.* You get to choose what you are drawn to and whatever you choose will be fantastic.

Another question that falls in the same category is what kind of tree to have. Some people like faux trees, some love live. Some people want a gorgeous show tree that is not to be touched, and some think the more homemade the better. Since I love each equally, I usually do one of each. I have a more formal tree in the living room that matches the room decor; then, when space allows, I place a red and green keepsake tree in the kitchen. If you don't have room for an extra, full-size tree, a small tabletop tree is a good option. So, know that whether you want your tree decorations to match your room decor or you feel like having a holly jolly classic Christmas treee trimmed with green and red, you made the right choice for you.

Speaking of choices, most of us have decorations that have grown old or tired. How do we know what is worth tossing and what we need for decor?

My tried-and-true method to determine which things to purge is to examine what you leave in your storage bins after you decorate with all your favorite items. If you didn't like it enough to put it up, it is time to throw it out. Everything left in the bins needs to go.

Remember That Decorating Is a Team Sport

The most effective way to tell the story of your family through your holiday decor is to include them in it. I actively brainstorm ways to engage my loved ones in special holiday fun. Fortunately, the holidays make this involvement almost effortless—both because of the importance placed on family and because the decor stays up for such a short season. These factors allow for taking design liberties that you might avoid if the results were on display all year. For instance, I do not want personalized stockings up all year, but since it is for only a season, it is totally doable.

I anticipate the moment when we unearth the decoration bins and start unpacking all the treasures from years past. I gingerly take out the tiniest miniature baby Nikes, hardly believing they once fit my oldest son's now-giant size eleven feet, and place those teeny sneakers among ornaments on the family tree. We go see Santa every year and turn the photo into an ornament. Yes, I still make my teenagers visit Santa, although they don't sit on his lap anymore. After all, everyone knows if they don't tell Santa what they want for Christmas, they might not get anything. Because my boys realize it is a treasured tradition, they are great sports.

Together, we fill the tree from star to stem with mementos, teamed with thick black-and-white velvet ribbon and round wooden frames of silhouettes of family members, keepsakes from a Disney World vacation. I don't want my tree to be so formal and untouchable that it's not personal to the people I share a home with. Many of the adornments have significance to us; among them, a time capsule scroll rolled in an ornament, forty-year-old keepsakes from my childhood tree (which is so strange because I'm pretty sure I am only twenty-seven), and handmade preschool relics my kids brought home as toddlers. While I think our tree is beautiful, I find it more important to fill it with precious memories that tell our story. Which is one of the ways I include my family in the holiday—the entire tree is made of *us*.

While we join together in person to decorate the tree, I don't want to paint an unrealistic picture of the actual day. This scene looks more like the Simpsons than Norman Rockwell. However, despite the complaints, this Family Fun Ambassador doesn't waver. Because I already know, based on real data by real scientists wearing real white coats, these times together will be some of the ones my kids look back on fondly. Even if they say things like "how much longer do we have to do this?" and "my friends don't help their mom decorate their trees" and "I heard this is what prison feels like." So, stay strong and fight through their complaints. Eventually, they will be glad you did.

Personalize the Holiday for Each Family Member

When my kids were younger, I put a small tree in each of the boys' rooms, decorated to match their room theme. My eldest had a sports tree filled with ornaments resembling basketballs and footballs, and my youngest, a Christmassy outdoor camping theme. Nostalgia washed over me when they unwrapped their trees, excitement sparkling in their eyes. They especially loved the magical look of the twinkling lights at night and asked to keep the lights on while they slept. Now they are older, but I still make sure to put some sort of Christmas decor related to their interests in their individual spaces.

Each year they unwrap a new ornament for their trees that will one day hopefully be the ornaments that start a Christmas tree for their future homes. Two special angel ornaments are designated for their future spouses, if they choose to get married, and each year when I unwrap them, I say a prayer that God will bless their marriages and keep them strong and healthy.

For some in the home, this could be including a plaid-clad tree in their spouse's study or a personalized stocking for their favorite pup. Personalizing a room does not have to be extravagant. It is a simple touch to include everyone who shares your space.

THE BUILDING BLOCKS OF CHRISTMAS DECOR

There is a reason some items are classic. Many typical Christmas decorations are underutilized and underrated. You don't have to employ an interior designer wholesale account to have access to the most useful components of Christmas decor. These are very simple items that most people have access to already. Yes, simple items are all it takes to make a room beautiful, and whether you are on a budget or decorating your seventh extravagant room, the most useful components are the same. I present you with my top five easy access, must-have items to decorate your space.

Ornaments

Ornaments are not just for trees. When decorating for clients and trying to stretch their budget, I stack them in a pretty bowl and set it on a table. It brings shine and texture, not to mention color. Placed in wreaths, nestled in garland, hanging from chandeliers, resting on each place setting—these baubles are a very inexpensive way to bring a little Christmas cheer to any surface.

Courtney's choice: Vintage lite bright ornaments

Garland

When we can utilize natural elements, we can bring the outdoors inside. Garland is one such adornment that goes the extra mile by fitting wherever there is a need. Appropriate in many locations, it freshens up staircases, mantels, and doorways. Lesser-known uses could be around chandeliers, media stands, and beds. Simple and green, or infused with berries and color, this is an item that makes the whole room feel festive. Some garland can stand on its own, some simply needs lights or ribbon and ornaments. A combination of all of these choices is a great way to make a room feel natural. Bonus: If you use live garland, it smells fantastic!

Courtney's choice: eucalyptus garland

Ribbon

Ribbon is the Christmas secret weapon and, again, it goes must further than placed on the tree or curled on top of gifts. Use thick and thin, wired and floppy, to vary similar but different hues and carry a color story throughout.

Ribbon provides a pop of cohesive color and has various uses:

- on the staircase in loopy bows or hanging with long tails
- around a wreath or candlestick
- tied to the back of dining chairs
- weaved through a place setting
- tied in a simple bow on the top of an evergreen tree

Courtney's choice: velvet ribbon in varied widths and shades of color

Small Trees

Even Charlie Brown knows that having a main Christmas tree is a given. But the real impact comes from placing small trees everywhere! Since decor looks best in odd numbers, I corral my trees in groups of three or five where I want to make an impact. Again, the element of a plant, whether real or a realistic faux, helps utilize natural decor and adds to the feeling of festivity.

Courtney's choice: a few tabletop trees from the local nursery

Wreaths

Once again, going beyond the obvious use for decorations opens up several options. Everyone hangs a wreath on the front door. But perhaps you could also display a wreath on the pantry door. I use wreath hangers and put them in numerous places throughout my home. (OK, let's be real. Every door in my house has a wreath on it during the holidays.) I love tying small ones to the back of a chair or setting one on china at a place setting. I also keep an eye out for them after Christmas, when things go on clearance, because no matter how many I have, I can always find a place for another or gift one to a friend.

Courtney's choice: find a wreath on sale after Christmas, then deck it out with decor from a favorite Christmas collection.

CELEBRATE THE SEASON WITH YOUR FAVORITE TRADITIONS

Christmas is an opportune time to tell the story of your family through the season. During a frenzied time of year, returning to a ritual brings peace that breathes air into my soul. In our house, we read the Christmas story from the Bible on Christmas morning, after we open presents. My kids' favorite tradition is usually making "Grinch Punch," a Sprite and lime sherbet concoction that we drink while watching *How the Grinch Stole Christmas*. On nights we are feeling extra spicy, we may drink it through a Twizzler straw, which is simply a Twizzler with both ends bitten off.

Not every tradition is centered around an activity though. Throughout the month of December, a standing hot chocolate bar sits in the corner of the kitchen, because nothing goes down as right as special late-night

Design Action Tip

Instead of decorating with fake snow, I use Epsom salt.

Then, after Christmas, I take down the ornaments, pour all the salt in the tub, and reward myself with a nice hot soak in the bath.

Okay, I don't really do that last part. But I could. And that's why Epsom salt is fun!

cocoa. Our Christmas memories book sits on the coffee table all month. This is a scrapbook that includes highlights from the year, photos, and our annual Christmas card. We complete it every year after the holiday, and now have twenty years' worth of memories. The kids marvel at old photos of themselves, usually prompting something insightful like, "Why did you let me dress like that?" which leads to me reminding them that they wouldn't let me choose their clothes at that age because they didn't want to do things like wear "pants with buttons." Bless it.

These are some of the rituals I have embraced during the holidays. Perhaps you could use one of the following to tell the story of *your* family throughout the season.

Display the Homemade Oven Mitt

Do you have preschool crafts from back in the day? Now is the time to dust them off and display them. There is nothing as cute as the crafts kids bring home from early school years, but I never know just what to do with them other than collect them in a box in the attic. The celebratory season is the perfect time to bring these handmade items out of storage and pepper them around the house. Place mats with painted handprints, ornaments with glued-on photos, popsicle stick photo frames, and the like are a sweet way to celebrate your childhood or your kids and tell their story, and likewise, remind you of beloved memories. I love glancing at photos of my boys with missing teeth and toothy grins as I move through the house and revel in the happy memories they stir.

Use the Fancy China

The fancy dishes never get much love. They usually stay packed away, perhaps to come out on Christmas day for the first time all year. In the spirit of celebrating the mundane, break out the fancy china and use it all December long. Even a Pop-Tart tastes better on a lovely dish.

Wear Matching Pajamas

Finding coordinating loungewear has gained popularity in the last few years, thus purchasing them has never been easier. When I started participating in this trend several years ago, I had to search around in multiple places to find various sizes that matched. Now stores offer matching sets in all sizes. So simple. The most difficult part now is convincing any reluctant naysayers to take part.

Host a Decorating Challenge

Challenge your friends or family members to a competition when decorating sugar cookies or gingerbread houses. (FYI, guys, I play to win. There will be no letting the kids claim victory in this house. I lose every basketball competition, but I make up lost ground when it comes to Christmas crafts.) I keep it super easy by picking up a couple of pre-boxed DIY kits or baking simple sugar cookies with my favorite ugly sweater cookie cutter. We lay out all the supplies, make sure to use royal icing because it spreads easier, and set up a time-lapse video on one of our phones. Afterwards, we relive the fun all over again when we watch ourselves decorate and bake in double time.

Honor Missing Loved Ones

My dad unexpectedly passed away from a heart attack in November several years ago, and our grief felt raw as we faced celebrating Christmas the next month with one fewer stocking on the mantel. When a parent passes away, you quickly join a club that no one wants to be a part of, but almost everyone eventually has to join. Despite our sadness, we made it a point to spend more time together through the month to help us process this crushing loss. That year, while shopping with my mom, I mentioned my obsession with glittered Putz Houses, saying that I have always wanted to begin a collection. (Putz Houses are mini homes made of paper and glitter that were popular in the 1920s–'40s. They are colorful and glittery

and delightful.) That Christmas, my mom gifted me one, bequeathed in memory of my dad.

Now every year when I unwrap the next piece of my growing collection, I honor his memory. I feel like this grouping of cheery houses is a small way to pay homage to his life during the season and remember him in a tangible way. Others may honor a missing loved one with a special ornament or by displaying a stocking with their loved one's name on it. It might be an adornment that memorializes the child lost in a miscarriage or an adoption that didn't get finalized. It could be a detail that no one else knows but those closest to you that helps you honor and remember the person you love and miss.

WHAT TO DO WHEN THE MAGIC IS MISSING

Let's be honest. In the real world, the holiday season doesn't always feel magical. Rarely does each year of life feel like we're the adorable main character in a Hallmark special. Real talk, there have been some Decembers when I honestly could not blame those non-decorating clients because I didn't feel like decorating either. (In the Hallmark movie, this Christmas Holiday Humbug would be the handsome and kind next-door neighbor who no longer believes in Christmas but has a beautiful singing voice and loves kids.)

During the years when it takes all my strength to muster a "Merry Christmas," I make it a point to find my cheer by turning my focus outside the home. Mostly this looks like serving others. The minute I begin to believe that my problems are severe, one look at what my neighbor is facing will back me out of the bitter barn. Serving others is an instant sobering fix to give us perspective.

Pay It Forward

One of my favorite lesser-known methods of serving is participating in the Silent Santa Game. Preparing for this secret mission turns you and your family into 007—Santa style—and it will turn any humbug into a true believer.

First, choose your recipient. Is there someone in your community who could use some extra care? Maybe this is a single mom who is burning her candle at both ends, an elderly man who doesn't get a lot of visitors, or a young family in the throes of exhaustion. Once you choose your target, the fun starts!

Every night for twelve days, deliver treats to their door under a secret identity. When we last did this, once we chose our recipient, my kids and I had so much fun buying small silly gifts, sneaking around, running away from the doorbell, and peeling out of the driveway so as not to be discovered. I knew my friend's schedule and even found a time she would be away from her house to leave her gifts. There are endless variations to embrace as you create the gifts—some people follow a theme and some simply leave a helpful gift.

We use the "Twelve Days of Christmas" song as a guideline to create clever riddles and rhymes but also to provide things we know our recipient needs. Because very few people have six geese a-laying on their Christmas list.

In an ideal world, this could be carried out with a delivery on the porch each night. However, since Christmas is the busiest decorating season in my interior design business, I know taking twelve separate secret visits during December would be difficult to uphold. In keeping with the belief that "the smallest act of kindness is worth more than the grandest intention," one year the kids and I packed up all the gifts in simple brown paper sacks with ribbon and labeled one for each day. We then left the entire package on the doorstep at one time, with instructions to open a gift each day.

At the end of the yuletide shenanigans, you can choose to reveal your identity or perhaps you may always let them wonder. I have included our daily rhyming cards, as well as instructions for how we did this, in the bonus materials of the book, found at courtneywarren.com/book. This is a delightful tradition that will be addictive for both you and those who do it with you, and it can reinforce your values, like:

We are a family that loves others.

We are a family that is generous.

We are a family that gives for the joy of giving and expects nothing in return.

The value of showing actionable kindness is worth more than a thousand lectures.

Facilitate an Impromptu Gift Exchange

How creative can you get? Take a friend, spouse, or group of kids to a mall or superstore and give them ten dollars to buy a gift for each other. It can be silly or helpful, given as one large gift or ten one-dollar small trinkets. The experience of finding the gift will be just as entertaining as the response to the reveal! To make it more interesting, specify that they have to wrap it with something they find for free in the store. (Toilet paper? Napkins? Marketing flyers?)

Maybe you came from a home that did not value traditions or simply did not have any. You have an amazing opportunity to create your own rituals for your family going forward. Meg Cox recommends first asking yourself, "What's the purpose of it? What do I hope my children and family get out of it?"[5] She says answering these questions will help give your tradition purpose, then you can make sure it is personal to the people involved. After all, the tradition should fit your family. Recently, a friend was asked what his biggest fear was about getting in a relationship. He quickly retorted, "Getting into a family that runs a 5K on Thanksgiving." Obviously, not every tradition will fit every person. One family might prefer something as simple as having coffee together on Christmas morning while another cooks breakfast for dinner on Sunday nights. You can easily tailor your tradition to fit the needs of your loved ones.

SPEAKING OF TREASURED MEMENTOS. Remember how thrilled I was to have a handmade artifact from my grandmother Elsie? After a closer examination of the place mats in my hand, I realized there had been some confusion. Unless my German grandmother christened her original creations with a Threshold tag that looked JUST LIKE THE ONES from a certain red-bull's-eye superstore. How strange. Upon the discovery of the tag, I called out my sainted mother as a big fat liar, because these treasured heirlooms from 1948 were actually from Target. (Now at least I know that love for Target is in my DNA. I got it from Grandma.) The oversight came about honestly, as my mom pulled the mats out of my dad's childhood box, probably mistakenly sorted some years ago. Always good sports, we all had a laugh when the mistake was revealed. So, for the rest of the night, when someone opened a gift that was obviously manufactured, like cowboy boots or a Patagonia zipper hoodie, we asked if Grandma Elsie made it. ☺

ACTION STEPS

TO CREATE YOUR CHRISTMAS STORY

Don't leave holiday connection to chance. Let these ideas empower you to purposefully engage in holiday traditions to keep your family connected in a meaningful way.

- Embrace classic Christmas colors or branch out for a more unique look—whatever hue you choose is allowed at Christmas.

- Display a formal tree, more casual tree, or one of each. The style of tree is whatever fits best for you.

- Determine what decor to get rid of by taking note of what is left in bins after you decorate your home. If you didn't want to display it, that is an indication that you no longer want it and can pay it forward.

- Display keepsakes from the past that you normally keep in storage.

- Don't overcomplicate decorating. If you don't know where to start, return to the five basics: ornaments, garland, ribbon, small trees, and wreaths.

- Encourage decorating as a team sport—don't allow humbugs to opt out of memories they will later treasure.

- Surprise a loved one with one more gift to open after Christmas.

- Make nights more festive with matching pj's.

- Break out the good china for this month.

- Forgo store-bought fake snow for Epsom salt instead.

- Create a hot chocolate bar and leave it out all season.

- Host a decorating challenge.

- Honor your lost loved ones with a tangible collectable displayed in their memory.

- Look for opportunities to find Christmas cheer by serving others.

- Create a new tradition with those you share a home with.

As soon as the Thanksgiving table is cleared, my design style morphs into "Christmas explosion." In fact, some people online think the after photo is of a Christmas display at a retail store.

Because my home serves me and not the other way around, I vary the room decor depending on my needs. Some years I display a decked-out, full-size tree, while other years, a tabletop tree does the trick. And when I need to keep it simple, I forgo both and allow the living room tree to take center stage.

I trim the chandeliers with garland and berries, display my Christmas signs, and unveil my collection of vintage Santas, scoured from flea markets and garage sales. This year, I added red throw pillows and blankets to the sitting area, and I housed a few vintage items under the table. A wreath holder hangs over the rounded pantry door and houses a cheery Christmas wreath filled with tiny kitchen utensil ornaments. I like variety, so I add different elements to my design, depending on the year. No matter what is ultimately displayed, I aim to make the holidays cheery and bright.

after

MEMORY LANE WREATH

Parenting—where the days are long but the years are short. Although I might have argued against that sentiment when I took my son to a high-end cosmetics store and he used the sample makeup applicators to clean out his ears. There is nothing that says "I don't get out much" more than the humiliation of buying a new lipstick while holding another human's used cotton swabs.

Setting aside those embarrassing mom moments, the years fly by and seem to speed up more during the holidays. I have mentioned my love of taking the kids for photos with Santa Claus. As we decorate, I savor unwrapping each photo frame like it's a miniature gift. I'm reminded of the circumstances of that year and the crazy events that surrounded the photo. If someone is squirming on Santa's lap, even better. The only thing more festive than individual framed photos is having those memories in one place! Cue the feelings and mom-nostalgia (momstalgia?) and let's make something beautiful!

Photos with Santa are how I commemorate my walk down memory lane, but this can be easily swapped for yearly Christmas cards, photos of your family, or photos of your pet through the years.

Want to make your own Memory Lane Wreath? It's easy!

Supplies:

- any type of hanging wreath
- photos printed in 2×3 size
- small photo frames (locker frames work for this too). A dollar store is a good source for these. Buy

more than you need so you will have matching frames for future years.

- zip ties (if the frames do not come with ornament hangers)
- any embellishments you want to add
- ribbon to make a big floppy bow (or you can buy a premade bow if you are "ribbon-challenged")

Steps:

1. Place photos in frames. Loop the zip tie around the photo frame leg, creating a small loop for a second zip tie to fit through.
2. Arrange the frames around the wreath in various places—some higher on the wreath, some lower. Leave space in the middle for a large bow.
3. Get the second zip tie, loop it through the zip tie on the back of the frame, and secure it to the wreath, pulling tight to fasten it.
4. Place any embellishments you want around the frames. These could be berries or springs if desired. But keep it minimal to let the photos take center stage.
5. Tie a big bow in the middle of the wreath. Hang it on the door with a wreath hanger and let all the nostalgia commence.
6. Add a new photo every year until the wreath is bursting with memories!

Conclusion

The Story of Your Home Is *You*

THE COLLEGE ARENA WAS PACKED with enthusiastic Baylor basketball fans, ecstatic that the team finally made the playoffs. When I attended college there, any sports championship was a long shot. When my date and I arrived late to the game, it looked as if there wasn't an empty seat in the house. Finally, I spotted a break in the faces of people. I motioned for my guest to follow me through the packed row, and we plopped down in the only two empty seats, thankful to finally sit and take in the action.

What I did not realize was that I was under observation. Twenty rows up, a friend watched as the scene that followed unfolded, and he knew something that I did not—there was a reason those seats were empty. He knew they actually were not part of general admission as I had assumed but were reserved and assigned to somebody. Even crazier, in a sea of tens of thousands of people from across the nation, those seats belonged to a person I knew, a person from my hometown. As my friend told me the story later, he saw a twist of fate that would be cruel if it was not so funny. He watched me lock eyes with the person whose seat I was sitting in. This person awkwardly moved down the row, and as I noticed him, all the blood drained from my face as what was happening began to dawn on me. The person I knew, the person moving toward me, the person whose seats my date and I had taken was none other than my high school ex-boyfriend, the one who had taught me the tough lesson of first heartbreak. In an arena that seated twenty thousand people, my date and I were sitting in the two seats that mattered most.

Our mutual friend watched this unfold from twenty rows up. He watched as I enjoyed the game, not knowing that my enjoyment would be short-lived. He watched as my ex-boyfriend scooted down the aisle to stand in front of me and say, "I think you're in my seat." He watched my face drain of color while I stammered an apology. He watched as I scuttled out of the arena with my date, trying not to shrivel up and die of embarrassment on the way to the parking lot. He watched it like a movie because he had perspective.

Perspective is a powerful thing. Sitting so far above the situation, this friend knew more than I did because I couldn't see what was happening in the same way he could. I couldn't see my ex-boyfriend standing on the bleachers, looking at his tickets and staring at me, figuring out that I was in his seat. I was too close to the situation and things were blocking my view. But my friend saw it all.

There's an overused business term that says it's good to have a "thirty-thousand-foot view." And that's what we have a chance to see now. We have the unique opportunity to imagine what we want our story to be. It's never too late to start again. As the Chinese proverb says, the best time to plant a tree is twenty years ago. The second-best time is now. Let us take the high view, look down, and determine how we want to tell the story of our families. How do we want our homes to feel, look, or smell? Do we want them to be full of joy? How do we put that in tangible terms? Let this moment of reading mark the time that you get your perspective that will transform your home for the better.

I want to offer you sincere congratulations. You've made it to the end of your design road trip. It's been quite an adventure, hasn't it? Are you leaving our journey together equipped with a few updated tools? (I hope so!) Did you come away with an idea of how to incorporate or better tell your family's story? Do you feel equipped with what you need to tackle a problem area, or do you have an idea of how to use a space in an un-conventional way? I'm excited to tell you that the most fun part is yet to come. Now you get to put your learning into action and make these ideas come to life in your home.

We've covered a lot of ground in this book, and as I stated in the beginning, different parts will apply to you as you go through various stages of life. In keeping with the mindset that "the smallest act of kindness is worth more than the grandest intention," I want you to choose one area of this book that resonated with you. I want you to brainstorm around that area and figure out what steps you need to take to complete that idea. Make a note in the chapter to go back and reread and underline. And then I want you to implement those steps in your home. Maybe you want to start incorporating more memorabilia in your bedroom so you add shadow boxes to your online cart. Perhaps you want to incorporate more of the senses in your living room so essential oils and fluffy blankets are on your shopping list. Maybe this year you're determined to make the holidays a little less stressful and a little more celebratory. Maybe this is the year you'll take out your grandmother's Christmas china and actually use it.

The most fun part is yet to come.

For some personality types, it's easy to get overwhelmed, declare that they've been doing it all wrong, and then throw out the proverbial baby with the bathwater. But hold on. There's still a baby in the bathwater. Let's save that baby. Rather, we shouldn't cast aside all good ideas because we can't do them all at once. Choose one thing now and then incorporate another idea in six months. Make notes as you go. Place a bookmark by what you want to do next, then revisit that page later when your phase of life changes. Go at your own pace. There is no rush. Every change you implement is another step toward better telling your story.

Remember my hope for you as you close this book? I want you to rise from your reading chair feeling empowered to create meaningful spaces that tell your story. So how about it? What is one problem area you now feel capable of conquering? What would it feel like to make a move toward the solution right now? What would that move be? What is holding you back from doing it?

Walking room by room through the house, we discussed practical actions to tell your story in each area. As a result, you are now driving your own pink convertible to your new destination, filled to the brim with fresh suggestions to try out. And like any good host, I will not let you leave empty-handed. I have compiled several bonus chapters as a thank-you gift to you, my friend who is reading this book. If you would like to gain access to even more premium material, just visit courtneywarren.com/book.

While all the ideas we covered are valuable, I want to remind you that your home has something that no one else can come close to: *You*. You are the most important inclusion. You are the centerpiece. The home is special because you are in it.

Have you ever built a model remote-controlled car? You piece each item together gingerly and secure it with glue. But until the power is turned on, the car will sit idle, no more useful than a statue. (I mean, I would assume this. I actually have never built a model car.) But you get it, right? We can fashion all the ideas and designs in the world, but without the life that only *you* can give your home, it is no more than an empty shell.

You are the magic unicorn.

You are the superpower.

You are the extra guac.

You. Yes, you.

You've set the goal for your home, and you are the captain at the helm of the ship. The love, care, and vision for your home are what breathes life into it and gives it personality. So, wield your power well. Take an idea you read and try it. See how it works. I bet you have more home skills than you realize.

Remember that typical design rules play second fiddle to surrounding yourself with things you love. Because when you mix in your special sauce, you will have a home with the spirit you dreamed of for you and your family, a home that tells a story worthy of passing down to the next generation.

Today is the day you get to begin telling your family's story in your home. And best of all, I already know it is a beautiful story, because it is yours. Tell it well.

Bonus Chapter

How to Secondhand Shop like a Pro

I AM A FIRM BELIEVER THAT A LOVELY HOME can be created on any budget, and one great way to stretch a budget is to shop second-hand. Most of my home's one-of-a-kind treasures and unique gems were purchased at garage sales. For someone like me who loves eclectic finds and vintage treasures, the only thing that could possibly be more exciting than to find a great item is to find a great bargain. Because I have years of experience, I consider myself a secondhand shopping expert. Whether you are shopping or hosting a garage sale, here are the most useful considerations to find great stuff on a budget—besides blenders and broken kid toys.

HOW TO SHOP A GARAGE SALE

Here are a few guidelines I follow when I stop and shop at garage sales.

Don't Pass Judgment from the Street

It takes effort to stop at a garage sale that doesn't look that great from the street. And sometimes I don't.

Sometimes all you can see is a box of rain-soaked Halloween masks and VHS tapes. But as long as there are a couple of tables filled with things I can't see, I make the effort to get out of my car and check it out. They might be borderline hoarders (garage sale jackpot) or even better, elderly hoarders (vintage find jackpot)!!

Research Multiple Sources

I follow neighborhood signs and also look on Craigslist. Online neighborhood groups are another great resource for finding upcoming sales as well. A couple of minutes of preparation can save you from driving up and down searching for signs and mapping out directions.

Skip Estate Sales

Surprised? These are usually put on by companies that tack on a hefty upcharge for organizing the sale. It is rare to stumble upon a great deal or an interesting find that is worth the price, which is usually akin to a fancy antique store. If I am going to shop at an estate sale, I wait until the last day when items are heavily discounted and are back to typical garage sale bargains. A great find can be had, but I would rather spend my valuable morning hours at other sales.

Make Your Hours Count

The earlier the start, the better the finds. Once you hit noon, things start getting picked over, and by two, people are usually packing up and calling it a day. Especially in the heat of summer. If you want to have the best success, set out early.

HOW TO HOST A GARAGE SALE

If you are hosting a garage sale, follow a few rules I have learned from experience.

The Name of the Game Is Realistic Pricing

Do not base your pricing on what you paid for an item or what it currently sells for in a retail store. Base it on what passersby could find at a thrift store and discount from there. Whether or not you used it, this item has been handled and you should price accordingly. They are taking a chance buying from a garage sale because if it does not work or fit, there is no return policy. If you are determined to get big bucks for an individual item, you should try eBay or a consignment store. Side note: Make sure your items actually have prices on them. Make it easy for them to give you their money.

Negotiate

If people want to negotiate, it is in your best interest to do so. Why? Because if you don't sell it, you will have to pack it up and haul it away. A little less money is better than hauling away something you no longer need or want. If the point of your sale is to get rid of your stuff, truly make it about getting rid of your stuff. Nothing is precious. It's a fire sale. Everything must go.

Don't Take Anything Back Inside

My rule is if you take it outside to sell, you are not allowed to take it back in. If you thought you didn't want it, your intuition was right. You don't love that item, and clutter will not add to the peace of your space. Take it to a charity and leave room for decor that delights you.

WHAT I SHOP FOR
AT GARAGE SALES

- vintage or pretty books to decorate a bookcase
- empty frames for a gallery wall
- anything with a story or history (Ask me about the card catalog in my house that has lived in both a library and a drug den!!)
- trays, baskets, containers

Bonus Chapter

How to Decorate around a Large TV

TVS SEEM TO BE A POINT OF CONTENTION, as it seems most clients I work with have a love-hate relationship with them. No matter our feelings about televisions, most of our houses have at least one, for better or worse. How do we embrace the eyesore they can create and incorporate them into our decor?

Mounted vs. tabletop: I prefer to hang the TV on the wall rather than set it on the table. When mounted with cords hidden, it looks cleaner and allows room for decorating around it, which minimizes its impact. The exception would be if you cannot place your cords behind the wall, then it is preferable to set your TV on the tabletop.

Here are three of my favorite ways to decorate around the TV:

1. *Make the entire wall, not just the TV, the center of focus.* Frame the TV with other items to be part of a bigger focus. Now it is just one part of a wall, with many interesting focal points.

2. *Keep it simple and minimal.* Mount the TV and include some colorful art nearby to infuse the room with the hues you want to complement.

3. *Utilize symmetry.* By flanking either side of the TV with the same items, the look stays clean and uniform. The TV is just one part of a streamlined space.

Whether or not we love the appearance of the actual TV, we can use one of these methods to provide a lovely look without ditching this source of entertainment and news. Which one would work best for your home?

Bonus Chapter

How to Combine Households

ONE OF MY FAVORITE MOVIES is *When Harry Met Sally,* and one of my favorite scenes is when their friends are merging their houses and arguing about keeping a wagon wheel coffee table. The man loves it. The woman does not. The man makes his friend Harry choose sides and is hurt when Harry admits the coffee table is ugly. Pouting, the friend says, "I thought you liked my wagon wheel coffee table." Already in a heated discussion, Harry yells back sarcastically, "I WAS BEING NICE."

Relationships, of course, require these little—and not so little—accommodations. Marriage. Remarriage. Boomerang kids returning home. Elderly parents moving in. You can be sure that whatever prompts the rearranging of your household to accommodate other people's tastes and stuff could also send you over the edge!

Now, my area of expertise is the interior design aspect of merging households. The solution of what to do about your adult child's love of blaring death metal rock at midnight is a question above my pay grade. But I'm sure you'll work it out!

For now, here are some tips I've found helpful when taking two households and combining them into one.

ANTICIPATE FUTURE NEEDS

Whether the decision to combine households was happily anticipated and desired or born of necessity, it will take some flexibility from all parties to make it work. Think and talk through the needs of everyone: privacy? accessibility? work-from-home space? When you know what will be needed, you can work together to make it happen. Remember, we are all on the same team.

BE PREPARED TO COMPROMISE

Blending households well, at its most basic level, is based on compromise. When one spouse is greatly invested in the home decor and the other feels mildly interested, the decision is easier. But how do you make decisions when both people have strong design opinions? In this case, I would look online first. If this is a clear-cut issue, someone in the industry is likely to have addressed it. Perhaps you can find advice that will serve as your tie-breaker. If that doesn't solve the issue, how can you compromise?

One client had a valuable sports jersey that one person in the family wanted to hang in a central location, but the other thought it looked tacky. I helped them brainstorm if there was a wall in the home that could work well for the jersey while staying out of the middle of the living room. Could your situation be worked out where both parties give a little and can feel satisfied with the results? If things get heated, remember the reason why you are merging households to begin with. There are reasons why you feel that living together is better than living apart. Honor the person above the design, and if you can give a little to make that person feel more satisfied in the home, your decision will be well worth it. If you absolutely cannot agree, call a professional or a talented friend. Someone with an eye for design can help you upgrade the space around the item causing trouble and perhaps find a way to make the most of it so both members of the house are satisfied.

KEEP WHAT YOU NEED, DONATE THE REST

I can tell you now that keeping duplicate items will likely clutter your space, so you'll have to decide what to keep and what to let go of (see

"Anticipate Future Needs"). To start, look through cookware, dishes, and small appliances, and keep the best. When it comes to the stuff of life, a big category is *sentimental items*. You must be brave. Sort through the keepsakes. Maybe you can integrate some family history into your new decor, as I did with my dad's sports memorabilia in my son's room. As for the rest, here are two options:

1. *Use this opportunity to purge what you don't need.* Pay it forward to a young couple or single who's starting to furnish a home. You could stage a pay-it-forward party for your family. Set it up like a garage sale and let them "shop."

2. *Find a worthy cause and donate your extras in good condition to them.* A domestic violence shelter that's setting up new homes for people starting over is a good place to start.

Most importantly, you're going for a coherent style in the merged home. Maybe there's a piece of furniture that you both decide could be repurposed in the new space. For instance, you can always make a chest into a TV console or a dresser into a sofa table. Maybe it just needs a coat of paint or new knobs to fit in (or make you not hate it). And, of course, good-quality soft goods can be reupholstered.

Sometimes you can merge personal belongings, such as art, by creating a gallery wall of your combined pieces. With decorative items that you decide to keep, you might try rotating pieces in so everyone's favorites get a chance to be viewed.

SHOP TOGETHER FOR NEW ITEMS

Sometimes, to get a unified look, you have to delete and add. Discuss the new look you're going for and set your budget for acquiring the larger new pieces.

Merging lives and homes can be done without bloodshed. And if anyone asks, no one likes the wagon wheel coffee table.

Honor the person above the design.

Acknowledgments

Ann Voskamp said, "When each woman shows up and does her brave thing, she actually wins a thousand other battles because she makes a thousand other women brave."[1] I am made brave by the women—and men!—who have gone before me, and I thank them.

First of all, I thank all who follow my social media accounts and blog. (Wanna join the fun? Let's rendezvous at my email list.) When I sat down to write this book, I had you in mind. Thank you for allowing me to speak into your life. I don't take that honor lightly!

To my family—Carolyn, Melissa, Rod and Gary, Trev and Trent, and families—a foundation of love and laughs is a powerful combination. Thank you for cheering on my unique gifts and providing me a wellspring of memories to draw upon. It is a joy for me to share our heritage with others. Thank you for being such wonderful sports to allow me to do so by sharing some of your stories as well.

To Mary who took a chance on a designer with a message and encouraged me to "write that book." You are a treasure who loves big.

To Kelsey Bowen who instantly "got" it when she heard my vision and graciously came alongside me to put it on paper. And to my team at Revell, I thank you for your tireless work of making me look good and sound coherent. Thank you for allowing me to have input in this process.

To my best friends, Kimber-Leigh, Shawna, Shannon, and Stephanie. It takes a village to be a creative mom, and you make it look easy. Thank you for the ideas in the section on ways to celebrate your people. I am honored to include your stories because not only do you have my heart but I think you are wise and lovely women whom we can all learn from. As Anne Lamott says, "In a very long time when we [all] go to heaven, we should try to get chairs next to each other, close to the dessert table."[2]

Thank you to Hilary Kennedy. Your white teeth still make me jealous, but I love your big heart and hilarious giggles even more.

To Joel, your belief in my early career taught me to believe in myself. Thank you for being the loudest voice cheering in my corner for so many years.

To my amazing clients who honor me by welcoming me into their spaces and trusting my vision to tell their stories. Thank you especially to Jason and Yessi Arismendi; Tony and Crissy Boyer; Candi Carney; Charles Cassady; Cory and Tracey Danner; Britney DeJesus; Brandon, Megan, and Kali Kleiman; Cody and LeAnn Herndon; Marina Foster; Sherri Mason; Terry McCabe; and Paula Waters.

To my photographers—Jarrod Estes, Shannon Williams, Chris Tucker, and Mandy Mann—thank you for making my designs look so beautiful.

To Debbi Garcia, who kept Courtney Warren Home running smoothly and kept our clients happy while I was away meeting book deadlines.

A few things brought me joy during the writing process and made life easier. To Culture Index, The Ticket 1310, and Diet Dr Pepper from Sonic, thanks for keeping this girl running at top speed.

To my boys, Judah and Abe, nothing matters more to me than you being a part of my story and giving you a story for the future. Our home would be empty without your voices quoting memes or your feet playing one v. one. I am proud of who you are and am so happy to be your mom. It is my best job.

To the reader of this book and all who might be new here, there are a lot of flashy things vying for our attention, and it is no small thing that you spent your time with me. Thank you for giving this book a chance. I truly hope you take away value for your home and, even more so, your heart.

Finally, it goes without saying that this book only happened because of not only what God has done in my life but also what he has not done. I do not know how to show my gratitude any better way than doing the best with what I have, and that is always my goal. So to God, I say the deepest, the most humble, the most honored, thank you. Always. Thank you.

Warmly,

Courtney Warren

courtney@courtneywarren.com
@courtneywarren

Notes

Introduction

1. Robyn Flvush, "The 'Do You Know?,' 20 Questions about Family Stories," *Psychology Today*, November 19, 2016, https://www.psychologytoday.com/us/blog/the-stories-our-lives/201611/the-do-you-know-20-questions-about-family-stories.

2. Cara Goodwin, "Could Sharing Your Memories Improve Your Child's Well-Being?," *Psychology Today*, April 4, 2022, https://www.psychologytoday.com/us/blog/parenting-translator/202204/could-sharing-your-memories-improve-your-childs-well-being.

Feature How to Start Your Story

1. Julie Andrews, "Do-Re-Mi," *The Sound of Music* (film), 20th Century Fox, 1960. Written by Rodgers and Hammerstein.

Chapter 1 Belonging Story

1. Stephen R. Covey, *The 7 Habits of Highly Effective People: Powerful Lessons in Personal Change* (New York: Free Press, 2004), 95.

2. Paul Simon, "50 Ways to Leave Your Lover," *Still Crazy After All These Years*, Columbia Records, 1975.

Chapter 2 Building Story

1. Janice Blakeley, "This Is STILL the Best Way to Design a Kitchen," Clever, February 15, 2018, https://www.architecturaldigest.com/story/kitchen-triangle-best-way-to-design-a-kitchen.

Chapter 5 Playing Story

1. Daryl Austin, "To Remember the Moment, Try Taking Fewer Photos," NPR, August 5, 2021, https://www.npr.org/sections/health-shots/2021/08/05/1022041431/to-remember-the-moment-try-taking-fewer-photos/.

Chapter 6 Celebrating Story

1. Anthony Silard, "Our Shared Loneliness," *Psychology Today*, April 4, 2022, https://www.psychologytoday.com/us/blog/the-art-living-free/202204/our-shared-loneliness.

2. Silard, "Our Shared Loneliness."

3. Silard, "Our Shared Loneliness."

4. Fazida Karim et al., "Social Media Use and Its Connection to Mental Health: A Systematic Review," *Cureus* 12, no. 6 (June 15, 2020): e8627, https://www.ncbi.nlm.nih.gov/pmc/articles/PMC7364393/.

5. Madeleine A. Fugère, "3 Effortless Ways to Become More Attractive," *Psychology Today*, April 6, 2022, https://www.psychologytoday.com/us/blog/dating-and-mating/202204/3-effortless-ways-become-more-attractive.

6. Belle Beth Cooper, "How Celebrating More Often Could Improve Your Productivity and Your Relationships," Planio, January 18, 2017, https://plan.io/blog/celebrating-productivity-relationships/.

7. Cooper, "How Celebrating More Often Could Improve Your Productivity."

8. Sebastian Ocklenburg, "4 Important New Discoveries about Hugging," *Psychology Today*, February 20, 2022, https://www.psychologytoday.com/us/blog/the-asymmetric-brain/202202/4-important-new-discoveries-about-hugging.

9. Priya Parker, *The Art of Gathering: How We Meet and Why It Matters* (New York: Riverhead Books, 2018), 216–17.

10. Mother Teresa, "Nobel Lecture," after the presentation of the Nobel Peace Prize, December 11, 1979, accessed August 23, 2022, https://www.nobelprize.org/prizes/peace/1979/teresa/lecture/.

11. @sitwithwhit, Instagram post, June 12, 2022, https://www.instagram.com/p/Cet2V5RuK84/.

12. Cara Goodwin, "Should You Call Your Child 'Smart'?," *Psychology Today*, April 6, 2022, https://www.psychologytoday.com/us/blog/parenting-translator/202204/should-you-call-your-child-smart.

13. It takes a village to be a creative mom. Some of these ideas were sprouted by creative women who love and celebrate their families well. Thank you for the inspiration, Keitha, Kimber-Leigh, Shawna, Shannon, Stephanie, and Sydney.

14. @justmadhu, Twitter post, July 9, 2021, 9:44 p.m., https://twitter.com/justmadhu/status/1413675464204472320?cxt=HHwWgMC–YeWsZ4nAAAA.

15. @donaldmiller, Instagram post, May 13, 2022, https://www.instagram.com/reel/Cdgt8HQMSL_/?igshid=YmMyMTA2M2Y=.

Chapter 7 Merrymaking Story

1. Rohini Venkatraman, "Science Says We Get Less Creative as We Age. Prove It Wrong by Doing 1 of These 3 Things," *Inc.*, May 9, 2022, https://www.inc.com/rohini-venkatraman/science-says-we-get-less-creative-as-we-age-prove-.html.

2. Meg Cox, *The Book of New Family Traditions (Revised and Updated): How to Create Great Rituals* (Philadelphia: Running Press Adult, 2022), 8.

3. Brett McKay and Kate McKay, "Creating a Positive Family Culture: The Importance of Establishing Family Traditions," Get Action, September 25, 2021, https://www.artofmanliness.com/people/family/creating-a-positive-family-culture-the-importance-of-establishing-family–traditions/.

4. McKay and McKay, "Creating a Positive Family Culture."

5. Cox, *Book of New Family Traditions*, 17.

Acknowledgments

1. Ann Voskamp, "Ann Voskamp—Thank God for Women," Vimeo, posted by World Relief, 2018, https://vimeo.com/296496380.

2. Anne Lamott, *Traveling Mercies: Some Thoughts on Faith* (New York: Anchor, 2000), 133.

Courtney Warren is a Texas-based interior designer whose work has been featured in *Real Simple*, *Better Homes & Gardens*, *Good House-keeping*, *Apartment Therapy*, and *Today.com*. She is a frequent consultant on Fox 4 TV's *Good Day* program in Dallas, was ranked in the top 3 percent of interior designers in the US by Houzz.com, and starred in the Dallas episode of TLC's *Four Houses*. She delights in helping overwhelmed clients create beautiful spaces and will never turn down a warm chocolate chip cookie or Diet Dr Pepper.

I would love for you to continue the fun. Please scan the QR code for bonus content, free gifts, and design tips. Or find me at courtneywarren .com/book.